CONJOINED

A Holocaust Haunting...
One Man, Two Hearts, and Me

a memoir by

KAREN L. KAPLAN

CONJOINED: A HOLOCAUST HAUNTING…
ONE MAN, TWO HEARTS, AND ME

Copyright © 2021 Karen Kaplan

Published by: Manora Publishing Company

Cover Design: Nevena Deljanin
Back Cover Design and Interior Typography:
Diane M. Serpa at GreyCatDot Digital Design
Editor: Mary L. Holden

ISBN: 978-0-578-92509-7 (paperback)

ISBN: 978-0-578-92510-3 (eBook)

Printed by Kindle Direct Publishing USA

First Printing: July 2021

"Anyone who has lost a parent, sibling, spouse, or another loved one knows how intense the pain and heartbreak feels. We wonder about the afterlife, and if our deceased loved ones are watching over us. In *Conjoined*, Karen Kaplan offers a firsthand look at communicating with the deceased through a psychic medium. What's so interesting and unique about this powerful page-turner of a book is that Kaplan uses the medium to talk to Arjei Kaplan, the deceased man whose identity was stolen by her father as a young boy in Poland during the Holocaust. I was amazed at the detailed stories Arjei Kaplan told through the medium. *Conjoined* offers readers a Holocaust saga, an understanding of how the past shapes a person's personality, and, the existence and power of the everlasting human soul. Kaplan writes with her heart, which makes her story even more captivating."

~ JACKIE PILOSSOPH
Creator and Editor-in-chief,
Divorced Girl Smiling
The Divorce Girl Smiling Podcast
Former Chicago Tribune *columnist, "Love Essentially"*

"Whether you believe in *gilgul* (the Kabbalistic concept of reincarnation) or not, this book is a beautiful story of one woman's search for *shalom* (the Hebrew word for peace, completeness). I enjoyed reading it and thank Karen for sharing an inspiring journey."

~ RABBI SHARI CHEN
Assistant Rabbi at Congregation Bene Shalom, Skokie, Illinois

CONTENTS

I dedicate this memoir to my grandmother Beila Szteinsaper (1896–1941).

She has been overseeing this project from the heavenly realms.

When her son, my father,

Avrum Szteinsaper,

witnessed the murders of Beila and his sisters

in his hometown of Rajgròd, Poland,

his whole life, and his name, changed.

Although Avrum Szteinsaper was stripped of his innocence,

my grandmother was thankful that Arie Kaplan survived the Holocaust.

FOREWORD

Karen Kaplan's *Conjoined* is an extraordinary memoir that combines a dramatic narrative of multigenerational trauma with an amazing journey of spiritual discovery. Its personal, detailed descriptions of an abusive household, and its account of suffering from a wide variety of perspectives make it universally resonant. Though the story emerges from a harrowing holocaust moment, its focus is on humanity and compassion, rather than inhumanity and rage.

Conjoined is not a typical book about the Holocaust and its effects.

I was truly moved and enlightened following Karen's personal journey from psychological injury and confusion to forgiveness. Haunted by the mystery of her father's double identity, she searched for and discovered the truth behind her father's behaviors and actions. She healed herself by reaching out to others, including the most unlikely souls. Karen came to understand her father—and herself—with the assistance of a psychic and channeler named Lea. The story of their relationship is astonishing, and yet it contains poetic logic. The relationship between Karen, Lea, and a certain troubled spirit is a mystical triangle where every side is essential to and supportive of the whole.

Karen's—and her father's story—is neither fairy tale nor fantasy. Her emotional strength and mission to know her parents, her religion, and herself is remarkable. She discovered that her father was even more troubled and unstable than she realized. During Karen's childhood, her family had been traumatized by domestic abuse, and as an adult, Karen was re-traumatized as she recognized the deep anguish of her father's spirit and how it had impacted her, her mother, and her brothers.

What I find most admirable is Karen's extraordinary courage in telling this very personal story.

The two of us met in a spiritual direction course many years ago. In that setting, I learned how to hold a space for another human being's spiritual exploration without judging their experiences or even needing to understand them on a rational level. But I did not have to suspend belief while reading Karen's story. She is neither gullible nor fanatical about spiritual and paranormal matters. She describes her own initial (and periodic) skepticism and astonishment with such directness and sincerity, readers can't help but be persuaded when she begins to take her paranormal experiences seriously.

I am certain most readers will identify, on some level, with Karen's traumatic childhood. Given the well-documented co-occurrence of trauma and paranormal experience, I think that many readers will also understand and be comforted by Karen's brave account of the strange ways she and Lea were able to connect the spiritual dots to find truth.

Though I have not had any comparable experiences, I found Karen's story to be compelling. It has truly changed my world view and my understanding of human relationships in general. Reading *Conjoined* has also given me a deeper appreciation of my friend—not in the least because I have come to understand her writing as a form of spiritual guidance. In an era where self-revelation has become confused with self-promotion, Karen's work shows the real value of the memoir—a deeply personal story to be read in quiet rooms and discussed with respect—and a dose of awe.

This is a sacred story, after all. Extraordinary and, on many levels, divine.

Christine Skolnik, Ph.D.
Alumnx, MFA in writing,
Vermont College of Fine Arts

CHAPTER 1

GETTING THE BIRD

ৱ

Bleeding hearts. Gardeners know these perennial flowers that bloom in the spring. Although their scientific name is *Lamprocapnos spectabilis*, their common name is exactly what they look like: red flowers in the shape of a heart with a 'drip' formation at their tips. The liquid 'blood' of this flower is conjoined to its solid 'heart.'

The Chicago Botanic Garden has several species of bleeding hearts in its collection.

On the day I was invited to speak about my first book, *Descendants of Rajgròd: Learning to Forgive*, to a group of women at the Chicago Botanic Garden, there were other kinds of bleeding hearts in the place. It's a public space—indoor and outdoor gardens cover 385 acres, including a cafeteria, yet these women were rearranging tables and chairs while other visitors walked about, carrying cups of coffee and breakfast trays. I was worried about standing up and bursting into speech that would carry beyond the group, but the organizer assured me that she'd gotten permission from the Garden's administrators to hold the event.

The ceiling-to-floor windows of the cafeteria faced a breathtaking view of a lake and the lush gardens outdoors. A few windows were open and the fragrance of late summer flowers in bloom enveloped us. As the women were rearranging tables, I noticed an older gentleman working at his laptop in the back of the room. Nearby was a young couple, eating breakfast. A female staff member, an employee at the Garden, sat adjacent to the windows, a walkie-talkie at her side, a clipboard on her lap.

I stood midway between two exits and watched people as they tossed garbage into trashcans and recycle bins, then stacked trays. It was noisy. There was no other place for me to stand; I was too distracted to review my notes. I could not find inner calm. It was disconcerting.

The group that invited me to speak consisted of women who'd emigrated to the Chicago area from Israel. They'd been meeting together for years and hosted monthly speakers for discussions about a variety of subjects. Because I'd been scheduled to speak before the Jewish High Holy days in early September, the women had invited me to discuss the theme of my memoir—forgiveness. After working on ways to understand the impact my mercurial, abusive father imposed on my life, I'd published that book in 2014 after decades of exploration. Emotional abuse during childhood affects decision-making, emotional well-being, and all relationships in a person's life. My goal in writing that book was to learn my father's background, understand how the Holocaust affected him, and then to forgive him.

The result of publishing *Descendants of Rajgròd: Learning to Forgive* was spending several years speaking at men's and women's clubs, libraries, churches, synagogues, college and medical conferences in Chicago, New York, Poland, and Germany. I've had the experience of applause—as well as audience members crying while sharing tragic life stories, and individuals waving their fists and criticizing my perspectives. Once, a woman stood up and rallied the entire crowd against me. The controversial topic of that book, and the tenor of the question-and-answer session discussions after speaking about it, provided me with feedback that was eye-opening.

I am the daughter of a Holocaust survivor, and I wrote about forgiving my abusive father as well as the perpetrators of the Holocaust.

The morning I was to speak at the Chicago Botanic Gardens, I woke up feeling queasy. I'd met some of the women before and knew that they represented a strong-minded group. I also suspected they would be relentless during the question-and-answer session. Like me, some of them were daughters of Holocaust survivors—and they tend to be among the most critical of my message of forgiveness. People who've experienced violence, war, and terrorism, whose husbands, brothers, sons and daughters have had to serve in the Israeli Army, who've had to fight for survival, have formed hearts too hardened to consider forgiveness.

To combat my anxiety, I prayed as I showered, dressed, and drove to the Botanic Gardens. I asked that this group would be open to my story, that they'd listen, hear, and receive what I offered, and, that they wouldn't yell at me. I didn't want to hear another person scream at me because I'd decided to forgive the Nazis for what they did to my family, my people, and all the world. Proselytizing is not my intention when I talk about my book. I want to share my story and explain what allowed me to move past my anger and to heal—it was so much more than conventional therapy.

The group had settled, and I started the speech with a greeting: "*Shalom*, and good morning everyone. It's a pleasure to be here, especially in the most beautiful gardens on Chicago's North Shore. Today I will share my journey of forgiveness and discuss the effects of intergenerational trauma on our lives."

A couple of people who were sitting in the back of the room were chatting. One of the Israeli ladies shushed them. At that same moment, the employee with the walkie-talkie who had been sitting in the back by the window stood up and looked at me. "Are you allowed to be here?" she asked. "This is a public space for all our garden members."

Before I could respond, the group's leader said, "Yes, I verified our meeting with the manager of the Botanic Gardens, and she approved."

The employee shook her head and sat down again.

I hoped that meant that the problem was solved and opened the story of my father's childhood in his hometown of Rajgròd in northeastern Poland. "He was born in 1921 to Chaim Shlomo and Beila Szteinsaper. Together with his five siblings they maintained a traditional Jewish lifestyle and lived in a two-story home overlooking the town square. His parents also owned a duck farm located a couple of miles down the main road. They were relatively prosperous. While I know that my father made favorable references to his youth in Poland, I regret that I don't have more specific information. I do know that he loved Eastern European Jewish and Polish foods and that he was especially close to his younger sister, Yoshpi.

When my father was a boy, his father died; a short while later, his 2-year-old brother passed away. Beila hired two local workers, named Kordash and Jablonski, to help manage the farm.

"The day my father's life changed in the most significant way is where this story turns dark. It was June 22, 1941. The Nazis invaded Rajgròd. With the help of German SS officers, the two workers from my grandmother Beila's farm forced their way into her home. From a hiding place, my father watched as they dragged his mother and two sisters, Yoshpi, and Leah, with her baby, into the yard. He heard how Beila was pleading for mercy—she begged to be killed quickly. She was slowly tortured and bludgeoned to death along with her daughters and grandchild. Helpless and anguished, my father ran away into the woods. He never looked back and never went home."

At this moment, an English sparrow soared into the cafeteria and flew straight to the glass wall. The bird fluttered up and down, trying to find a way out. I kept speaking, but like everyone else, I was distracted.

The staff member stood up and I heard as she spoke into her walkie-talkie: "We have a situation in Room A of the cafeteria. Have someone come quickly."

"Ladies," I said before turning to Hebrew, "*sheket bevakasha*. Please, quiet down. Someone will be here shortly."

Unlike the bird, they settled. I continued. "My father was filled with bitterness, resentment and anger and vowed never to be a victim again. Even though he immigrated to Chicago, met my mother, created a family and began a new, comfortable life, he could never forget those gruesome years. He hardened his heart, his anger became uncontrollable, and he abused my mother, brothers and me."

A large man with bulging biceps entered the room, saw the bird, and spoke into his walkie-talkie, "Hey Johnny," he said, "we need a bird net stick. Pronto."

One of the ladies from the group told him to pipe down, and he snapped, "Hey lady, don't tell me to be quiet. I'm working here."

My plan was to get the man's attention and avert a fight. "Please go ahead and do what you need to do," I said, "and I'll continue speaking." Within minutes, a young guy arrived carrying a six-foot metal stick with netting on the end, which I assumed was the "bird net stick."

Sounds of clang, clang, clang reverberated—it was the stick banging against the windows. The sparrow kept flying—upwards and downwards—avoiding capture.

I felt bad for the scared little bird.

A woman from the group stood and yelled, "Can't you figure out how to do this quietly?"

The muscled man turned to her and hollered, "What are all of you doing here anyway? You are not allowed to have a function in this public space!"

The group leader pointed her index finger at him and yelled, "It's none of your business. We have permission to be here!"

A few more ladies stood up to defend her. One cried out, "We've done nothing wrong! We don't like the way we are being treated!"

One woman howled that she was going to go straight to the supervisor and end her membership with the Chicago Botanic Garden immediately.

"Ladies!" he screamed "I want all of you outta here!"

I was still standing at the front of the room where I could see everything that was happening. "Sir," I said in a loud voice, "sir, your partner just caught the bird. Please, I'll be finished in a couple of minutes. Then we will all head out to the terrace!"

"You better put the chairs back the way you found them," he replied.

"Of course we will," I said.

The two of them took the bird and left. The women—upset by the interruption—buzzed up the volume, venting their anger.

"Please, please, calm down, ladies," I said. "Let me finish talking about forgiveness and how you can attain peace and joy in your lives."

Now I see it as kind of funny, but I couldn't quiet them down. I was frustrated. The women left the room fuming and yapping on their way to the outdoor terrace. Once we reconvened, I rushed through to the end of my story. There were only a few questions and a short discussion, then we were out of time. Everyone left.

I sat outside, alone, looking at the tranquil waters of the lake, taking in a few deep breaths, enjoying some personal peace.

Another English sparrow flew past where I sat. It made me laugh as I realized those angry women never directed any rage at me. They'd spewed it on the Chicago Botanic Garden employees. This little feathered friend had answered my prayers.

While driving home, I called my good friend Lea and told her the story of how the speaking event had gone, and how the bird saved my pride. I knew she'd understand.

Lea started out as a psychotherapist and evolved into a spiritual teacher, medium, and channeler. She's self-confident, insightful, and unafraid about confronting people with their innermost truths. We met in 2008, and over the years she helped me realize that my upbringing had damaged me. It was Lea who helped me to come to terms with my father's broken past and its effects. I had written my first book with her encouragement.

After I mentioned how a tiny bird had flipped my speech, Lea snorted and we both found the laughter. She's tiny and soft-spoken, and she snorts when she laughs. But, when Lea speaks, everyone listens. As our conversation continued, Lea said, "Karen, do you remember the first time we met?"

I did. I'd gotten her name from my close friend Ross. He is a remarkable therapist and well-known expert and author on narcissistic personality disorders. Ross told me about a patient who came for an appointment one day—after a few sessions she was doing remarkably well. He was stunned to see how this uptight, unhappy woman had transformed to someone who was now smiling and relaxed. The patient explained that she'd met with Lea, who'd helped her get to the core of her issues, a deep-seated fear stemming from her childhood. The patient had never brought it up in any of her sessions with Ross.

Ross gave me Lea's card, so I called her. That was the way we met, and from a few words in, I knew she was someone who could teach me. Lea told me she channeled information from spirit guides and was able to offer people insight because of the information she receives. I was curious about how she did it and wanted to know how she'd helped Ross's patient heal.

I also wanted someone to help me heal from an abusive childhood with a damaged father.

Lea was comfortable leading a group session and told me that she would be in the area on a certain evening, so I invited her to my house to talk about spirituality to friends and family members who were open to a different way of looking at life.

Everyone gave their full attention to Lea as she spoke. She held their interest until the end of her talk when she said something that seemed out of place: "Your

Jewish community has been through a long history of suffering and pain and now it's time to heal."

We were stunned. I felt like she'd come into my home and weighed in on matters about which she probably knew nothing. Lea had grown up in a small midwestern town and lived in an area where there were few Jews and no connection to a Jewish community. I thought it was bizarre for her to speak like that about my people, and I saw that some of my guests were uncomfortable. I felt as though she'd insulted us, and I didn't think our paths would cross again. But, after a few months, I realized that Lea had seen something I could not see. I called her and ended up going to see her for two years of private sessions. She opened my eyes to a way of thinking I'd never considered before, and taught me that there are no coincidences, that life gives people what we need, and that there are reasons for what happens in each life. Beyond therapy, Lea became a close and valued friend.

I said to her, "Of course I remember the first time we met, because you upset some of my guests in my home and I couldn't wait for you to leave."

"Well," she said, "today you witnessed first-hand how your community is still afflicted by the Holocaust and continues to carry the pain and agony of decades of war in Israel. Their anger is bubbling up to the surface and can easily ignite and turn like a wildfire out of control."

She encouraged me to remain detached from the outcome as I continued to speak to audiences that could be volatile or reject me. And she told me that she was proud of the work I was doing.

A sense of pride. There's something about being told that you've made someone proud of you. I remembered how my mother used to be proud of me while my father never managed to share his feelings or give me a compliment.

I told Lea that the trapped English sparrow reminded me of an ancient custom involving a bird that some Jews still follow around the time of the Jewish High Holy days. Just before Yom Kippur, the Day of Atonement, they twirl a live bird, usually a chicken or rooster, three times over their head. A prayer would be recited then the fowl was slaughtered and given to the poor to cook and eat. The purpose of the custom was to transfer an individual's sins onto the bird so that one could begin the new year with a clean slate. I was grateful that my father, in spite of all his other issues, never followed that custom.

Lea said she was glad the sparrow didn't suffer any more harm than I did. Then she snorted again, and we both laughed.

CHAPTER 2

SOMETHING SANDY SAW

২

I was still in a state of grief a year after my mom died. It was 1998, and I'd sob whenever I watched a mother holding her toddler or saw a mother and daughter shopping together. When I was at the grocery store, I'd be wondering what my mom might have been cooking that day. She would often prepare extra food for my family. I still had containers of her chicken soup stored in my freezer from the year before. I just couldn't use them, nor throw them away.

It had also been seven years since my oldest brother, Howard, died unexpectedly, at the age of 35. I never stopped missing him.

Wondering if they were both watching over me, if they saw my three children growing up, or if they were resting in peace were constant thoughts. Near the end of my mother's life, we had a brief conversation about the afterlife. I remember crawling into her hospital bed and wrapping my arms around her. She kissed me on the forehead, and I felt her love even though she was lethargic and highly medicated from pain pills and chemotherapy. I asked if she believed in life after death and she said that she didn't think it existed.

We'd never discussed it before, and I was surprised that she was so definitive about it. I felt sick to imagine that my mother would die, and I'd never see her again. I was crying because of that finality. I hadn't spent much time thinking about it, but I'd learned about the soul, and had always counted on the soul being immortal. I said, "There has to be more than just our existence. If there is an after-life, I imagine you showing up for graduations, bar mitzvahs, and weddings." At that moment, I realized a need to hold onto this belief because without it, I'd feel all alone in my world.

After she died, I became obsessed with the idea of talking to my mother again. I kept noticing psychics and mediums on television talk shows promoting their newly released books and talking about their abilities to communicate with the dead. Some also provided messages to audience members about their deceased loved ones, and I wanted to be one of those people who received a message. It seemed real, perhaps because I was so anguished about having lost my mother, but I couldn't stop thinking about communicating with her.

I wanted one of those mediums to transmit a message that only my mother would know, like about how she used to take me downtown on the bus and subway, and we'd shop at Marshall Fields on State Street, or see a play at the old Goodman Theatre on a Sunday afternoon. Afterwards, we'd go to The Berghoff, a restaurant, and my mother would enjoy watching me devour shared slices of German choco-late and Black Forest cake. I loved our time together because it was just the two of us without my brothers or father around. Would a psychic be able to tell me about how, before my mother and I left to go downtown, she would take cash out of her purse and stuff it in her bra? I then imagined how the psychic would describe my mortification whenever my mom would stick her hand down her shirt to retrieve some money to pay the bill.

But I was raised as an Orthodox Jew and talking with a medium was taboo.

From a very young age, my father was adamant that we keep kosher and attend services every sabbath and holiday. During my 12 years of private Jewish day school education, I studied biblical and modern Jewish history, orthodox doctrine and traditions, and the Hebrew language. My unyielding loyalty to Judaism made life simple because all the rules were predetermined, and it was just like following the procedures of a manual from start to finish. We weren't required to understand the rules, but my father insisted that if we didn't observe every last rule, he would punish us. I was obedient and rarely misbehaved, but I remember my brothers getting whipped with a belt for skipping a Saturday morning service. My father thought that by following the rules, we were ensuring the survival of our people.

My family life along with my schooling was focused around a millennium of suffering and annihilation of our people, including the six million Jews who were murdered during the Holocaust. My identity as a Jew was defined by fearing and confronting the effects of antisemitism that had coursed through the veins of generations of my people. That fear shaped my relationship with Judaism and God.

That fear was also partly the reason that instead of seeking a medium, I decided to have a conversation with my rabbi. I was so heartbroken in grief over my mother's death, but I also felt a sense of spiritual emptiness and loneliness in my marriage. My three children were young, and observing the many orthodox rules left me feeling bogged down and unfulfilled. As I grappled with my religious upbringing and wondered whether I should continue that way of life, I was just too afraid to make any drastic changes and transgress the laws. I was still hearing a voice that threatened God's or my father's wrath if I should stray. I was raised to revere rabbis and their teachings, so I realized that my only option was to ask my rabbi.

So, I sat in the rabbi's office and blurted out that I was desperate to communicate with the spirits of my mother and brother and wanted to see a psychic medium. I admitted that I was preoccupied and anxious, I couldn't focus on my work, and I'd become impatient with my family and friends. "Is there life after death?" I asked him.

Was it odd that I was hoping for his approval? Was this the beginning of a rebellious stage? Or was I hoping that the rabbi would say something inspiring to encourage me to keep the laws? Would he sense that I was feeling lost and ask me about how I was coping with my loss? I wished I'd thought it through more carefully and hadn't also admitted my desire to see a medium. Part of me hoped the rabbi would see my anguish, but I'd forgotten that he was even more attached to the rules than my father had been. It would have been nice if he'd noticed my anguish and said something soothing or encouraging.

What he did say was: "It's heresy, Karen, contacting the dead is prohibited." Then he opened a book of the Bible and read to me. "Leviticus 19:31: You must not turn to mediums or spiritualists, do not seek them out, or you will be defiled by them. I am the Lord your God." The rabbi turned to another page and read, "A man or woman who is a medium or a spiritualist among you must be put to death. You are to stone them; their blood will be on their own heads."

Of course I knew that and was ready with a response. "King Saul sought out the witch of Endor to conjure up the spirit of the prophet Samuel. Doesn't that suggest that there is life after death?"

The rabbi was silent for a moment and then responded, "Focus on life, not death." He glared at me.

How could I tell him I needed more than that as an answer? I wanted to hear that the afterlife is just another form of the human life I was living, and that there was nothing wrong with trying to communicate with the spirit of my mother. It had been drummed into me from an early age to want the rabbi's permission, and now I realized that it was never going to happen. What was so terribly wrong about communicating with the dead?

I left his office and ignored the rabbi's reply, disregarded the words of the Torah, and went to seek comforting words from a close cousin of mine. I told her that I wanted to find a medium who had a direct line to the other world, and she put me in touch with a well-known medium in the Chicagoland area.

The medium's husband answered my call. He explained how to prepare, and how the hour would flow. I mentioned that I'd never done anything like this and that I wanted to communicate specifically with two people who'd died. The husband said that his wife, Sandy, could not guarantee who might show up during the reading.

That would have been amusing had I not felt so broken-hearted. I asked if it was possible that nobody would show up from beyond the grave.

The husband said that if no spirit came, I wouldn't have to pay.

I found that comment to be funny because of course the spirits would want me to get my money's worth!

Sandy's husband assured me that a spirit had always shown up, without exception. I should have been calmed by that, but then I shared my worry about seeing a medium because I'd grown up believing it was forbidden. He said if I was uncomfortable then I should not meet with Sandy.

While he was talking, I realized that the urge to talk to my mother had become so strong that I was going to go ahead and meet with Sandy, even if it meant being spiritually cut off from the Jewish people. I told him that I was ready to schedule an appointment for the following month.

Before we ended the call, I said, "I know this might sound silly, but what do I wear to see Sandy?"

He laughed and said that I could wear whatever I pleased.

In my mind I pictured this medium wearing a long and flowing colorful skirt with a puffed sleeve blouse, a head scarf and large, gold, dangling earrings and many necklaces. She would be sitting behind a tiny table with her hands placed on a glowing crystal ball.

On the day I met Sandy, she was dressed in a casual blue and green floral wrap-front dress that was knee length. She welcomed me into her little office far out in the northwestern suburbs of Chicago. A little stand-up fountain bubbled in the corner. I noticed a few framed pictures of spiritual quotes on the walls and a lit eucalyptus scented candle was on her desk. There was spiritual literature and a signup sheet for her class on developing intuition and psychic ability on a nearby console table.

We sat across from each other at her desk and she asked, "Can I hold something of yours that you touch every day? Car keys would work. Feeling your energy helps me focus on you and the reading."

I handed her my keys. I was nervous about what might happen and skeptical that nothing would happen. I sat there with my arms crossed and showed no emotion on my face. I did not want to give off any responses to affirm or deny her comments, and I was surprised when her initial warmth seemed to fade, and she spoke to me in a businesslike, clipped way. Maybe it was because I was acting so reserved, but I'd expected a little more compassion.

She reached across the desk and asked to hold my hands. She closed her eyes, so I did the same, and then she gave a brief Christian prayer asking for protection and guidance. I masked my discomfort with the prayer because I hadn't told her that I was Jewish. She might have been more sensitive had I been more upfront.

I took a notebook and pen out of my purse.

Then she said, "Your mother is here and standing at your right side."

Unconvinced, I didn't say anything while I wrote what she'd said in my notebook.

Sandy continued, "She passed away roughly a year ago."

I didn't move a muscle to deny or confirm what she said.

"She died soon after she was diagnosed with cancer."

Now Sandy had my full attention. My mom died within six weeks after being diagnosed with a rare form of uterine cancer. By the time they found it, she was already in stage four and the cancer had metastasized throughout her body. My dad had never been good about taking care of any of us, and after mom went into the hospital, he visited her a few times a week while my brother Barry and I stayed at her side until the end.

The medium then accurately described my mother's health issues, my father's inattention, and their relationship to one another. "If you feel a slight tickle on your cheek or the feeling of a bug in your hair, just know that it is your mother communicating with you. She wants you to know that she's with you and your children."

I thought I was sitting as still as a mummy, but I ran my hand absentmindedly through my hair as if I felt that bug. I was starting to wonder why Sandy knew so much. I felt my heart pumping and hoped she couldn't hear it. I nodded my head and she continued.

"There's a male energy present that has passed and is standing behind you. He was young. He seems like a brother. He is holding a Bible and standing on a pulpit. I see a Jewish star. Was your brother a rabbi?"

"Yes." I responded with an impassive, still face. My voice might have been the tiniest bit shaky, but I've been told that my poker face is really good.

Sandy talked about my brother's physical height (he was six-foot-six), his love of God, his devotion, and how sorry he was for running over my leg with his bicycle when I was seven.

Now my fingers were clammy and my neck was tingling. When my brother ran over me, I ended up in the hospital with twelve stitches on my leg. She added that he'd taught me how to drive a car, which was true.

The hour flew by quickly, and I was vacillating back and forth between believing her and thinking that she was a fraud. I said, "It seems like you could have easily found some of this information on the internet. I'm not fully convinced."

"Karen, I see dozens of clients each week and I'm not about to research them, their friends, and their relatives. Nor am I going to memorize all their backgrounds and medical histories. If you don't believe what I'm saying, that is your prerogative."

As I sat there mentally reviewing what she said, Sandy added one final piece of information, "Your mother sends well wishes to your relative who is in the hospital with a dog bite."

Now I let my jaw drop and widened my eyes. My breathing was ragged. That week, my cousin's dog was hit by a car and when she ran into the street to comfort her dying dog, it bit her. The wound became infected and she was hospitalized. There is no way Sandy could've researched that on a computer.

"Karen, we're finished. Please pay me," she said as she held out her hand, clearly wanting me to leave quickly.

I seem to have a knack for making great first impressions. It took me six months to get another appointment because she refused to allow me back into her office.

But I was persistent. I begged her.

She relented.

The second visit went better. I apologized for doubting her and I was more receptive.

During our third visit, after she'd finished channeling my mother's spirit, she chatted with me. It was a little surprising because we hadn't talked like this before, and I'd been curious about her life. I said something about how grateful I was to have found her, and she said, "When I first met you, I wanted you to leave my office as soon as you walked in."

I smiled because I remembered being reticent and skeptical. "You were completely closed off, energetically," she continued, in what I thought was a nice way of saying that I'd been bitchy. "But my spirit guides told me to keep working with you. They knew that eventually you were going to embrace this new way of thinking."

I asked if she could tell me more about life beyond death and about spirit guides. She explained that we all have spirit guides, or universal forces of energy that accompany us throughout our lives. Their mission is to assist us in our life journey and help guide each of us to grow into the best person we are meant to be. These spirits can also warn us of impending danger and comfort us during challenging times.

I didn't realize we had just one guide let alone several. I asked her if she knew who my spirit guides might be.

"The prophet Samuel is one of your guides," she said. "You will be receiving a sign so that you will know this is the truth."

I had a bunch of questions to ask, but it was time to leave. What kind of sign was I supposed to look out for? Maybe I'd spot a billboard or an airplane banner in the sky with an advertisement for Samuel Adams beer, or maybe I'd come across an "Uncle Sam" poster. I was becoming leery and thought this whole spirit guide thing was far-fetched. Doubt was building. Everything Sandy had said made me wonder if I had been conned all along. Had I mentioned the prophet Samuel to her, or to her husband when I first called? I put myself in her shoes and decided that for several hundred dollars a session, I'd do a little research if I wanted to impress someone about what I knew.

Just a couple of days after my third session with her, my eldest son Max, who was 11 years old at that time, asked me for some help with an assignment. All my children Max, Noah and Raquel, attended a private Jewish elementary school. Max always excelled as a student and had never once asked me for help in any of his classes. But now he said, "We just started studying from the Book of Samuel and I can't understand the Hebrew questions."

I froze. Chills spread up and down my entire body. I thought this was probably the sign Sandy had been talking about.

Then I recalled Sandy's spot-on comments during our three sessions, and in that moment, I was thoroughly convinced that there is life after death, was sure that Sandy could connect to it, and positive that we all have spirits guiding us in life. I was also beyond grateful that I could simply call Sandy, my medium, make an appointment with her and have a direct line to my mom. To this day, I'm still blown away to think that I can talk to my departed mother and she can respond.

After the deaths of my brother and mother, I couldn't stop thinking about who I was and why was I still alive. My introduction to this unseen, unscientific and foreign world helped me delve further into other questions like, am I just a speck of organic particles that breathes and dies? Is there a purpose to my life? The questions made me realize that I'd been feeling empty and spiritually hungry to know more. I needed to explore and understand what happened in my life to stop me from moving forward. The insights Sandy gave me took me to a whole new world, offered me a sense of direction, gave me a path to finding my purpose.

After building this relationship with Sandy, I began telling the story of my spiritual journey to others, with hope that it could bring comfort and hope to those who'd also lost someone. I had not believed in it at first, but as I explored this new world, I discovered things that changed my thinking and secrets that gave me insight into people I loved.

Now, I want to reach out to those who have lost their sense of purpose, those who wish to understand their past, and those who always suspected that there is more to this world than we can see. I understand that some may doubt my story. If you're one of those skeptics, then consider this book as pure entertainment; as being in the paranormal, science-fiction category. Either way, sit back, relax and let me welcome you to my world.

CHAPTER 3

MY NEW MILLENNIUM

ॐ

The old century was in its final hours. What we called "Y2K," or 2000, the new year of the millennium was about to arrive. Fears regarding glitches and interruptions in computer systems had spread across the globe, but I was watching Dick Clark on television as he announced the countdown to midnight in Times Square. Two million people had gathered to watch, all standing shoulder-to-shoulder from Central Park to 42nd Street to watch the ball drop. People were partying like it was 1999. And it was.

Earlier that day, I'd read that the White House staff had created a time capsule of the 20th century that included a photo of Rosa Parks, a piece of the Berlin wall, and some film from Neil Armstrong's walk on the moon. They'd stored this time capsule in the National Archives and Records Administration and announced that it would be opened in the year 2100. Inspired by that story, my children Max (11), Noah (7), and Raquel (5), and I put together our own time capsule with a plan that it would be opened in 2025. After we'd decorated an empty, extra-large sized popcorn tin, we placed our new year's resolutions, artwork, poems, and toys inside the capsule. I added the front page of the December 31, 1999 *Chicago Tribune* newsletter, and sealed letters I'd handwritten to each child. We sealed the capsule shut with duct tape and I stored it in the attic of our home.

The new millennium motivated me to rethink my typical new year's resolutions of shedding a few unwanted pounds and adhering to a solid work-out regimen. I decided that 2000 was the year I was going to work on my emotional health. I needed to bring some joy into my life. Even though it might have seemed like my husband and I were leading happy, successful lives, our marriage was falling apart.

I was mentally and emotionally drained from doing everything I could to avoid seeing him or engaging with him. When he was working in the den, I went into the basement to play with the kids, or upstairs to do housework. If he went to bed first, I'd wait until he fell asleep. I'm not even sure if he noticed; it felt like I'd gone way down on his list of his priorities. He was busy building a medical practice, reading the weekly medical journals, or playing tennis and working out to relieve stress. As his wife, I had fallen by the wayside. It felt similar to what I'd experienced as a child—being ignored, unappreciated, and feeling unloved by my father.

Over those years, I'd talked with many women who had experienced similar feelings. They'd distanced themselves from their husbands by sleeping in separate bedrooms and taking separate vacations. I knew it was only a matter of time for me because I saw each one of them experience divorce.

Divorce didn't seem like the best option. I still wanted my husband to accompany me and my children on Saturdays at the synagogue, and to be part of that community of friends. I wanted us to have a better bond, to be a happy, loving couple. But I didn't know how to solve the problem.

My unresolved feelings towards my husband became more pronounced when my mother died. My mom was my support system. She was the only person in the world who had my back; who loved me unconditionally. After she died, I felt a huge hole in my heart and realized that my husband wasn't able to help remedy my deep grief. We lacked the emotional connection that such a task required. I just couldn't see a future with him.

Edith Eva Eger, Ph.D., a psychologist, author of *The Choice: Embrace the Impossible*, and Holocaust survivor, wrote, "We don't marry our parents, we marry our unfinished business."

Clearly, I needed to learn from that relationship and my role in its demise. Maybe if I had been upfront early on and told my husband how I felt, things might have turned out differently. But I avoided confrontation.

At that time, I didn't understand the impact of my childhood on my adult life. As I reflect back on my early years, I realized that my adult behaviors mirrored my childhood ones. The way I coped with my father was to make myself invisible and to keep clear of him whenever possible. By maintaining a low profile as a child in my family's home, I managed to avoid much of the household drama he incited.

As a married woman, when I nonchalantly suggested marital counseling, my husband was not interested. I would not go to see a marriage counselor on my own. I didn't think it would help us anyway, so I was happy when he rejected the offer and I began to wrestle with the idea of getting a divorce. The overwhelming fears of being on my own, and raising three young children, were too much for me to handle. Though I was hoping that the new millennium might encourage me to move forward, my hopes for happiness were put on hold. I wasn't sure if I could make that transition...at least not yet.

Still, I was taking baby steps to make some changes in my life. When I was young, I was insecure about my body size and was picked on at school. I was very tall and *zaftig*, a term used to describe a plump raisin. Shopping for clothes was challenging back then because there were limited choices in my size, but I always managed to find a few outfits at a store on Devon Avenue called Chubbettes. Imagine how embarrassing I felt telling my friends where I bought my clothes.

When I was in middle school, my mom took me to a dressmaker where I picked out patterns and material for skirts, pants, and dresses for the bar mitzvah parties I'd been invited to attend. I loved that she wanted me to look my very best. At those parties, slow dancing with boys who came up to my chest gave me some of the most awkward and self-conscious moments during my pre-teen years.

At that same time in my life, my relatives advised me that drinking coffee could stunt my growth. I consumed large amounts of hot coffee, loaded with milk and sugar. Perhaps it worked. I wouldn't want to be taller than I already am, even now.

At five-feet-ten inches tall, I was a half inch taller than my husband. I always felt insecure when standing next to him. I tried slouching, but that looked worse. Wearing flat shoes during our marriage wasn't always what I wanted to do—but I did. At my wedding, I wore ballerina flats made of white lace so that my husband and I would look perfectly matched when standing side-by-side under the *chuppah*.

But now at the new millennium, I was emboldened to buy shoes with one-inch heels. And, as the new millennium advanced, I graduated to wearing three-inch heels toward the end of 2000. In some small way, wearing heels gave me a sense of liberation. Those new shoes were for me—not for us. When my husband noticed that my heels were higher, he took out a tape measure to check their height, and then he knew our marriage was in serious jeopardy. He had tried making some efforts toward reconciliation by helping out with the kids and the housework, but our problems were beyond his well-meaning attempts.

I knew I needed to do something other than buy more high heeled shoes.

Since Sandy opened my world to a new way of seeing things, I started reading all sorts of metaphysical books about near-death experiences, chakra healing, and spiritual growth. Then I joined a study group at the Kabbalah Centre in a nearby town. Kabbalah is an ancient form of Jewish wisdom that reveals how the universe works. I learned about the path of the soul, reincarnation, and dabbled in the practice of meditation.

A new friend from Kabbalah class suggested that I attend a 10-day silent meditation retreat called Vipassana. Vipassana is an ancient meditation technique that has been handed down since the time of Buddha. It literally means seeing things as they really are. My friend said that the retreat had helped him immensely.

Ten days away from my children seemed like a lifetime, but I had to do something soon because I had just experienced my first anxiety attack at home. It was on May 4th, our anniversary, which also happened to be my husband's day off from work. That morning I dropped my children off at school and drove back home. I assumed my husband would be working out at the health club for a while so I would have time to gather my things and leave the house before he returned. I didn't want to spend any time alone with him, especially on that day. As I pulled into my driveway and opened the garage door, I saw his car. At that moment I worked myself into a frenzy and began breathing heavy and gasping for air. My hands were clammy, and I gripped the steering wheel as if it were a life jacket, keeping me afloat in the water. I thought I was having a heart attack. Panicked with fright, I sat in the car until my breathing normalized.

Then I was able to drive away.

During the rest of that year I opened up and shared my thoughts with some friends about getting divorced. The conversations were fine, but some of their unsolicited advice is what made me more upset. One of my girlfriends told me that unless my husband was physically abusive, an addict, or an adulterer, I should remain married to him. Her parents divorced when she was young, and the event damaged her childhood. My father warned me to stay married. He seemed so angry and said that he wouldn't help me out financially if I should need it. Another girlfriend was planning to call my husband and attempt to reconcile us, against my wishes. I managed to stop her.

During those disheartening times, I was also considering the possibility of leaving my synagogue, a community where I had raised my children for almost 10 years. I met some wonderful friends there, but I was feeling less connected to the religious dogma. Services were uninspiring and my prayers felt empty. I was worried that my friendships might end.

One friend, who was becoming more religious as I was feeling more disconnected, suggested that I see a psychiatrist. A friend since our high school days said that she was concerned that her Jewish community, a few suburbs away, would frown upon her for maintaining a friendship with me, should I become a non-observant Jew.

Feeling bogged down with all this emotional turmoil, I realized that I needed to quiet down the chatter in my mind, let go of my irrational fears and be present to make the hard decisions ahead of me. After months of consideration, I decided to sign up for the Vipassana meditation retreat. I made all the necessary arrangements for my children to be cared for while I was away. My in-laws gladly helped with carpool and watched the kids after school until their dad came home from work. A few other parents kindly offered to have sleepovers for them during the weekend. Before I left, I wrapped a few special gifts for each of them along with some "I miss you" cards and left them on their beds. Then I drove a couple of hours through the flat plains of central Illinois—it felt like the middle of nowhere—to the Vipassana retreat center.

The place was surrounded by soybean and corn crops. The accommodations were sparse, but I was given a private room that had a standard single bed, a small wooden desk, a wobbly chair and a tiny closet. The walls were beige and bare, and I felt lonely. Down the hallway was a communal bathroom for all the women on our floor.

At registration, the leaders were friendly and helpful and welcomed all 60 participants. For the next 10 days I had to surrender myself to the teacher, the discipline, and the teaching. I had filled out the necessary forms and signed a code of discipline with an exorbitant list of rules to follow.

After day one, I was ready to quit.

Something made me stay.

In the back of my mind, I wondered if I had joined some kind of cult. I'd worried that I'd made a huge mistake. I wanted to let go of the rules—not add more to my life. I was prohibited from talking, reading, writing, and listening to music. There was to be no looking at others, no use of technology, no sex, no drugs no alcohol, no working out, no stealing, and no killing.

The no killing rule was difficult. On day six, I saw a grossly ginormous centipede crawling up and down the wall in my room. I barely screamed and instinctively grabbed my shoe to throw at the creepy crawler. Then I remembered I'd vowed not to kill. I ran out into the hallway and noticed that the other women had opened the doors to their rooms and were looking out to see what the commotion was all about. Embarrassed, I quickly walked down the hallway looking downward, avoiding eye contact, as I went on my mission to find one of the assistants for help. Were all my fellow retreatants looking downward too? I didn't know. Fortunately, I recognized a pair of shoes that a leader was wearing and led her back to my room by motioning my hands. She grabbed a cup and a piece of paper and followed me back to the room.

She removed the insect while respecting its right to live.

Each day, wake-up was at 4:00 a.m. at the ring of a gong. A half hour later, I was sitting in a meditation hall with all the attendees. The room was always dimmed but as my eyes adjusted to the darkness, I noticed the high ceiling, wood paneled walls, dark hardwood floors, a fireplace and the out-of-date floral curtains covering the windows. We had designated spots on the floor and cushions to sit on that were available nearby.

For 10-and-a-half hours each day I learned to meditate by listening to a taped recording of a man named S. N. Goenka. The first three days involved observing my breath as it entered my nostrils and noticing all sensations in my nasal region. The silent part was tedious, but I have always breathed through my mouth because I have a deviated septum. After those three days, and for the remaining seven days, I worked on breathing through my nose and concentrated on skin sensations on different parts of my body. I still don't know how I managed to stick with the intense breathing exercises and rigorous mental training for the entirety of the retreat.

Sitting on the floor, remaining still as much as possible, was also unbearable. I couldn't stop moving my legs and arms. I felt like I had the extra-hyperactive form of ADHD for the first few days. My back and neck muscles tightened. It was painful to sit upright for long stretches of time each day.

There were two meal breaks each day for breakfast and lunch. I sat in the dining hall looking downward and staring at the vegetarian food. Others sat nearby. No one spoke. At 5 pm there was an optional tea break, with biscuits. It was the highlight of my day because they gave me several flavors of tea to consider. Repeat students were only allowed to drink lemon flavored water in the afternoons.

On the third day of meditation exercise, as I was going deeper and deeper into the practice, something out of the ordinary happened. My mind seemed to be going insane. I had no control over it. It felt like I was in an operating room, laying on the surgeon's table without anesthetics, being sliced open. I felt exposed, and very helpless. I was truly scared and didn't understand what was happening.

By the fourth day, my mind shifted. It went completely blank. It was the strangest feeling I'd ever experienced, yet, it was so comforting. I could feel my entire body—it was in a state of bliss. I noticed my energy as it went coursing from my head to my toes. My mind and body were in sync and completely relaxed. I could not recall that I had ever felt this calm.

The remaining days of the retreat seemed to fly by quickly. Now I felt truly happy and content—with not a care in the world. Wishing the feeling would stay with me forever, unfortunately, it ended a few weeks after the retreat.

Once the euphoria left, I observed how sad I was in my marriage. That extreme level of happiness gave me contrast and made me see that I was depressed. The Vipassana meditation helped me see things as they were and also allowed me to tune in and trust my gut instincts. Now I knew that divorcing my husband was the right decision. I also recognized that my children would be fine, as long as they were nurtured and surrounded by love.

At the end of 2001, our divorce proceedings began soon after Max's bar mitzvah. My husband moved out of our home. We signed the divorce papers one year later.

My spiritual journey continued after the divorce. I met with all sorts of healers, some who were charlatans, and others who understood me. First there was Daniel, a palm reader, who compared me to a moth that is drawn to the light. As the moth flies closer to the flame, it eventually backs away for fear of being burned. He understood my desire to be in a loving relationship with a man but the fear of getting hurt or rejected was holding me back.

Daniel's advice made me recall that while growing up, I witnessed my mother suffering terribly while married to my dad. I didn't have any role models for a healthy relationship. I became adamant that I was not going to repeat my mother's way of life. I vowed to never let a man disrespect me again. But I was too scared to open myself up to possibly getting hurt. Daniel made me realize that I had a great deal of personal work ahead of me.

Then there was John, a Sufi master and an aura reader. He was tall, and extra-large, with a Buddha-like belly. There were always strings of wooden mala beads around his neck. His thin, long, blonde hair was pulled into a ponytail, and his sparkling hazel eyes seemed to pierce into my soul when he read my aura for the first time. We were at my home.

John explained that by studying a person's aura, it gave him valuable insight into their mental, spiritual, and physical states. He gazed directly at me, and around my body. He noted a dullness and sensed that my energy was flat. He asked me, "Karen, are you happy in life? What is it that you really want?"

My reply was along the lines of how I loved being a mom and enjoyed working at the neighborhood vitamin store. I was able to maintain a small private practice counseling men and women in nutrition and wellness which helped pay my bills. But I still felt troubled by my religious upbringing and felt disconnected with my synagogue community. I also shared that I was determined to find love—not marriage.

"On the surface," he said, "you appear happy, but there is no passion in your life. Love is not found externally. It begins inside of you. You can find love with a dog, Karen. Your chi is weak and is making you tired because you are not excited about life."

His words hit home. "How do I create excitement?"

He said that it already existed inside of me. Then I remembered from the Vipassana retreat how invigorating I felt as energy—my chi—was rippling through my body. I looked at him, searching for more.

John reiterated that the excitement would appear when I got back in touch with my inner self, but something was still holding me back. "Hold out your arm," he said. "I'd like to do some muscle testing on you. This helps me tap into your sub-conscious mind, to gain additional information about you."

I willingly stretched out my arm and held it parallel to the floor. He placed two fingers on my wrist and pressed down as he asked me all sorts of questions. He focused on my responses by how I resisted or gave in to the pressure.

He stopped asking questions. Concentrating, he continued to apply pressure to my wrist. After several minutes had passed, he said, "You have built up anger and resentment toward your tribe. You've allowed them to control you. You have put your community needs ahead of your own. Yet without them you feel you cannot survive, and you fear being shamed by them. This internal struggle is weakening you. It needs to be resolved before you are able to move on."

"What can I do?"

"I feel as if there are old Jewish souls lingering in this house. You've made a deal with them. If you obey their sacred laws and pass them down to your children, then they will protect you," he said.

"But where am I without my community?"

"Pursuing your own path in life doesn't mean that you need to disconnect from your tribe."

I thought about what he had said and then told him to sit tight while I ran downstairs into the basement. After a few minutes, I returned with a three-by-two-foot painted ceramic sculpture of three old ultra-orthodox rabbis in black suits with prayer shawls and *kippot*, head coverings. They were all hovering over the Torah. My great-aunt Dora had made this piece of art for me years ago. She was a grandmother figure for me after my mom's parents died. Aunt Dora had stood up at my wedding. I loved her dearly. I'd kept her gift as a reminder of our close connection, but it scared me. I'd stored it away in a closet in the basement because I couldn't give it away.

John looked at the gift and said, "Are you ready to break the contract with these old Jewish souls, regain your independence, and create a healthy connection with your people?"

I nodded yes. He took the art and asked me to follow him outdoors onto the driveway. As we stood outside, he handed it back to me and said, "Tell these rabbis what you feel."

Those painted clay rabbis were close to my face as I looked directly at them and said, "I'm removing the shackles that have bound us together. They no longer strengthen me. I do not serve you or your religious doctrine. I am taking my power back. Our contract is null and void." Then I lifted the sculpture over my head and threw it onto the cement pavement. The rabbis shattered into hundreds of pieces that scattered all over the driveway. I felt like Moses may have felt when he stood on Mount Sinai in the act of destroying the first set of the 10 Commandments. It felt liberating.

Then—a warning! John said, "They won't give up so easily. You will be challenged in the future. Stay aware."

CHAPTER 4

IT'S NOT KOSHER

ॐ

Keeping kosher is one of the rules of the Torah that I had followed for decades, yet there is no explanation behind this law. Only animals with split hooves that chew their cud are permitted for consumption. Eating pork is prohibited. Fish and seafoods are required to have both fins and scales, so lobster, crabs, mussels, and clams are all taboo. Kosher animals must be killed properly and completely drained of blood because blood is strictly forbidden to consume.

What I never understood was why from the 12th to the 16th centuries, some Christians accused Jews of killing Christian children and using their blood to bake matzoh for Passover. This libel about blood taken from dead children spread all throughout Europe and Jews were massacred because of the lies of Christians.

I'd kept kosher all my life. Going to McDonald's and ordering a hamburger was never an option for me. Mixing dairy products and meat products together is not permitted; I had never eaten a cheeseburger or a steak with a glass of milk. In my home were separate pots, pans, and flatware—one set for meat, one for dairy—to ensure that these foods would never mix.

Keeping kosher was becoming laborious and uninspiring.

I shared thoughts like this with my buddy Ross. He is a secular Jew. Ross and I act like siblings, but without the drama of competition and antagonism. Ross often shares his personal problems with me and asks for my advice, which I consider an honor.

I could never be a therapist because I do not have the patience to listen to someone repeating their same old problems. I'd be drained. But, when I was in the midst of separating from my husband, I became tired listening to myself *kvetch*, a Yiddish word that means habitual complaining. It caused me to shift my way of thinking, and I decided to focus on the positive aspects of getting divorced. As a result, my friends, along with many acquaintances at the gym, now come to me with their issues. They know that I am well-meaning, honest, and blunt. I never give advice based on what I would want, but by understanding their past issues and their personality, I share my thoughts. I always tell my friends upfront that I am not a therapist, that I may not side with them and that I won't be insulted if they choose not to listen to me. They often tell me that their therapist gave them the same advice as I did.

Once, while talking with Ross about my "kosher problem," I decided to do the unthinkable. Ross and I scheduled to meet for lunch at Carson's Ribs, a restaurant in my hometown of Deerfield, Illinois, the following day. We met in the restaurant parking lot where I donned a black hat and sunglasses. I began feeling the knots forming in my stomach but forced myself to open the car door and walked inside with Ross.

Ross said "You don't need to go incognito. No one here keeps kosher and wouldn't care what you eat." But I had reminded him that I'd kept kosher my entire life, that eating pork was the epitome of transgressing God's law and that my community would frown upon me.

Inside, we were greeted by the hostess and I had requested a corner booth in the back of the restaurant. Ross smirked and suggested that I could take off my disguise, since there were no one else sitting nearby. I removed my hat and sunglasses and immediately opened up the extra-large menu and slouched behind it. The waitress asked what I'd like to drink. I said I needed something strong. Even though I hardly ever drink alcohol and am a total lightweight, I ordered a cosmopolitan. Ross ordered a Heineken.

When she returned with our drinks, she asked us what we'd like to order. I said, "Ribs, I guess."

"Which ones?" asked the waitress. I didn't know there were different kinds of ribs. Ross took the initiative and ordered spareribs for me and baby backs for him with extra barbecue sauce on the side. Then she handed us plastic bibs and Ross immediately tied his bib around his neck. I didn't.

"Aren't you going to wear your bib?"

"No," I replied. "There's a pig dancing on it."

"If you believe that keeping kosher is the right thing to do, then by all means follow the laws. Whatever you decide, do it for yourself," he said.

"I'm here. And steadfast." but I was kidding myself. I was hesitant and unsure if I could ever break this law. If my father knew that I was eating pork, he would curse me and then he'd cut me out of his will. Then I wondered what God might do to me. But I grudgingly put on my bib as the entree was placed in front of me. I stared at the ribs for several minutes while finishing my cocktail.

Ross dipped each single rib into the sauce, then devoured them with great enjoyment. He then licked his fingers clean. When he noticed that I had not touched the food, he used his fork and knife to cut the ribs on my plate into individual pieces. "There, that will be easier for you. Grab the end of the bone and dig in. The meat is quite tender and will easily fall off," he said.

My forehead and the back of my neck were sweaty. I was feeling lightheaded. Was it the cosmopolitan, my nerves, or maybe a bit of both? I slowly picked up a rib and held it between my fingers. I stared at it for another few minutes, took a deep breath, closed my eyes and bit into it. I chewed and chewed that pork rib very slowly. I couldn't swallow it…not just yet. There was still some time to spit the masticated meat into my napkin, I thought. Another minute passed. I forced myself to swallow it. I looked over my shoulder thinking I might see a bolt of lightning ready to strike me down. Nothing had happened and I was relieved. God had not punished me. Or so I thought. I smiled and said, "Not so bad." I ate a couple more of those spareribs and managed to finish the side of coleslaw. Then I wiped my mouth and fingers clean with a wet towelette that the waitress had given me. I squared my shoulders and perked up. My inner self felt liberated at having accomplished this colossal act of defiance. It was like a huge load was lifted from my shoulders and I felt lighter.

During the next year, I acted like a child in a candy shop. I went to eat at McDonald's, Burger King and Wendy's. When dining in upscale venues, I ate steak and chicken. Seafood reminded me of large arthropods and I just couldn't eat anything that resembled an insect. The fear of being ridiculed and judged by my friends had slowly diminished and one by one I began telling them. Those who disapproved of my actions, soon fell to the wayside.

At that time, my brother Barry, who was living in California, called me. His voice sounded very jittery as he said, "I have something very important to share with you. I'm not sure how you are going to react." Then he admitted that he'd eaten chicken in a restaurant.

I had burst out laughing and couldn't stop. He realized that I, too, had stopped keeping kosher. What a coincidence. We both were relieved to bring this secret out in the open.

After a year of practically eating fast food every day, I was feeling lethargic and having severe pain on the right side of my abdomen. The pain began shooting up my back, so I went to see my doctor. She said, "You have acute cholecystitis. Your gallbladder is inflamed, and you have several gallstones. You will need to have your gallbladder surgically removed." She handed me a surgeon's card and wanted me to call him as soon as possible.

"God is punishing me," I said under my breath.

"Excuse me, did you say something?" the doctor asked.

"It's not important. What if I don't have the surgery?"

"Sepsis can occur, and it is quite dangerous," she said.

"Thank you," I said, and left.

As a nutritionist, I knew that the high-fat, fast food diet had caused the condition. I needed to make healthy changes to reverse the diagnosis. So, I detoxed my liver and gallbladder with a cleanse, the gallstones flowed right out of my body. I started juicing, eating tons of vegetables, and adding a few fruits. I limited chicken and fish and removed all red meat from my diet. Three weeks later my energy level improved, the pain had subsided, and I was feeling a whole lot better. I tore up the surgeon's card.

If God had punished me, I had found a workaround.

As a reward, I decided to use some money I'd saved and left for a solo two-week trip to Europe while my children were attending summer overnight camp. It was at that time when I implemented a new dietary rule—it was to eat healthy and leave room for a little chocolate.

My kosher days were over.

CHAPTER 5

TO HAVE, TO *GET*

ॐ

About a year after our divorce in 2004, my ex-husband called to ask: "Will you drive into the city to the Chicago Rabbinical Council and apply for a *get* [a Jewish divorce]?"

"No, thank you" I said, "I don't live my life according to the authorities of the rabbis anymore and I certainly do not need your permission to remarry."

"But I would like to have the *get*. I will need one if I remarry. I want to follow the rules properly," he said.

"Why would I drive all the way into the city for you? Where were you when I needed you?" I said. What chutzpah, I thought. Yet I was proud of myself for speaking up to him at that moment, something that I rarely did when we were married.

"Give it up already, Karen," he remarked, "you're certifiable."

"I'm not going to sit in a room of rabbis dictating what I can or cannot do and be humiliated for an afternoon. It's not my idea of enjoyment. And to add insult to injury, I'm not going to pay them hundreds of dollars," I said.

"I'll pay for it."

"Not interested." At this point, I could tell he was very annoyed.

"Well, I would like to get this done. If I pay for the *get* and ask the rabbis to come to your home, will you sign the papers?" he asked.

"Fine," I answered, but with reluctance.

It was so strange to me—hearing him verbalize his loyalty to the Jewish laws. All throughout our marriage, I wanted him to be part of my religious life with our children, but he wasn't interested. When we divorced, I distanced myself from religious life, and he embraced it. The children were a bit conflicted and didn't know what to make of the ways their parents had swapped religious lives. I told the kids that the beauty of life is that people can change at any moment in time. "Today you may believe one way," I said, "and tomorrow you may decide another way works better for you. In the meantime, when you're with your dad, respect his wishes and keep kosher."

One week later, three ultra-orthodox rabbis all wearing black suit jackets and pants, white shirts, large black hats, with full beards and lengthy, curled *peyot* [sideburns] were walking up the driveway. As soon as I saw them through the windows in the foyer, I gasped. My legs began to shake, and I leaned against the front door. They reminded me of the spooky three rabbis from the sculpture that I had destroyed right there on the pavement under their shoes.

I recalled John's warning that I need to stay aware.

When I heard their knocks, I took a deep breath, stood up straight and opened the door. They introduced themselves and I invited them into my home. All three men took seats across from me at the elongated dining room table. The head rabbi was in charge of conducting the ceremony, while the other two men were the official witnesses. All I could offer them was water in bottles and paper cups because my home was not kosher.

One of the witnesses said, "This is a huge dining room table. It must be nice to have holidays here. Do you celebrate a kosher for Passover?"

The head rabbi was preparing the documents.

"Yes," I replied. "I invite family and friends for the holidays. We celebrate the important message of freedom from slavery, but I don't keep kosher for Passover. I'm pretty certain that Moses would not have approved of today's countless dietary rules. He came down the mountain with only 10 commandments."

The head rabbi interrupted and said, "We will commence with the divorce proceedings. Your ex-husband applied for the *get* last week and authorized our scribe to handwrite this legal decree. He has declared of his own free will that he is giving you this *get*."

I was annoyed and insulted at hearing that my ex-husband was "giving" me this so-called gift of freedom. He was not my master, nor was I his slave. It was 2004. I could not believe that women had allowed themselves to be treated this way. "This *get* is futile," I thought because in Israel, my girlfriend had been waiting years for her husband to sign the *get*. She could not remarry until she had it. She could not receive government aid because she was still considered married, despite the fact that she was raising her children on her own. Her husband had moved out. I had heard that in certain religious Jewish communities on the East coast of the United States, some women needed to pay a group of men to beat up their husbands and force them to sign the *get*. Otherwise, they were endlessly trapped in their miserable marriages. It was so sad to me that these women were bound to a set of rules that continued to make them feel like victims.

After the rabbi read the twelve-line decree in Hebrew, he said, "Now I will read the English version."

"That's not necessary. I understand Hebrew."

He said that there were set procedures for this ceremony, and he kept reading. When he finished, he folded the paper meticulously several times into smaller squares, then triangles.

"Hold out your arms," he said. "I will drop this into your hands."

"Why?"

"So that you formally acknowledge that you are willingly receiving this *get*," he said.

I was reluctant to follow his wishes. I felt pressured to hold out my arms. In the end, I cupped my hands together and he dropped the paper into my palms. He was careful not to touch me.

I looked and felt like a beggar, asking for a handout. This *get* was not my sustenance nor was he my savior.

"Now raise your arms over your head," he said.

"And...why?"

"To make sure there is no other document up your sleeve," said the rabbi.

My eyebrows scrunched downward. I pursed my lips. "This is crazy," I thought. "A simple signature would suffice!" Still, I accommodated the rabbi and lifted my arms up high. Then immediately I withdrew my cupped hands and placed them on my heart. I told him that it felt much better there.

He paid no attention to me. "Now stand up, put the paper under your arms and walk three steps."

Anger was building inside of me and my body temperature was rising. "Are you kidding me? No, thank you, rabbi. I've had enough."

I respectfully handed him the *get* and he took a pair of scissors and cut a slit into it. "This *get* has been delivered and accepted. It cannot be used by any other party and will be placed into our files," he proclaimed.

I was hoping the ceremony had ended, but the rabbi continued to speak, "Now you must adhere to two prohibitions."

"What are they?"

"If you plan to remarry, you must wait 92 days from today."

"How did you derive that number?"

"If you happen to be pregnant, it would help us determine who the father might be."

"Genetic testing would resolve any unanswered questions. I don't think there is anything to worry about because I haven't slept with my ex in years."

The rabbi's face was expressionless. "In regard to the second prohibition, you are not permitted to marry a *kohain*."

A *kohain*, or the plural *kohainim*, were priests serving in the first and second Holy Temples of Jerusalem over 2,000 years ago. To this day, men who carry this prestigious lineage, which many believe cannot be proven, are given special status in the synagogue and follow certain restrictions. They are prohibited from marrying a convert or a divorced woman because they are required to maintain a level of holiness and purity that exceeds the rest of the people. They are also restricted from having contact with corpses, so many will not walk onto a cemetery or walk under a tree that overhangs from the cemetery onto the sidewalk.

Now my upper body muscles were tightening. My eyes were narrowing. I could feel my face turning a deep shade of red. I understood the rabbi was doing his job, but I couldn't handle any more directives from him.

"Rabbis. If I want to marry a *kohain*, I will do so. I'm not tainted. If I want to marry a non-Jew I will do that as well. None of you…I repeat, none of you…can mandate who I will or will not marry. If I choose to get married next week, then so be it!"

They looked a bit surprised. Quickly they collected their documents and walked to the front door. The head rabbi said, "May we see you in better times."

"These are the good times. I appreciate you taking the time to come to my home. Thank you for today. It was an empowering experience."

I opened the door and watched them walk down my driveway. I felt free.

When I was younger, I assumed that people who were older than me like my parents, teachers, and rabbis were wiser and knew what was best for me. When I realized this was far from the truth, it was time to take responsibility for the direction of my life. My ideologies had crumbled before me as I started letting go of the archaic, fear and shamed-based rules one-by-one.

Over time I began listening to the small voice inside of me and learned to trust myself more and more on what felt right in the moment.

CHAPTER 6

AN UNHEALED HEART CRACKS FURTHER

క

March 19, 2013 was a cold, windy day. Even in my warm house, I still felt the chill of winter. I was upstairs in my bed, wearing pajamas and a robe, under the covers, watching television. Two of my children were home on spring break from the University of Illinois. It was 11 pm. My son Noah was studying for the MCAT exams in the kitchen. He was wearing headphones, listening to a lecture on his computer. Noah dreamed of becoming a doctor, and that's how he was spending his vacation. My daughter Raquel had just kissed me goodnight and gone to her bedroom down the hallway.

Having dozed off, I didn't hear what happened next.

Three masked men stormed into our house. They yanked Noah out of his chair and threw him to the ground. He landed face down. They zip-tied his hands behind his back. They zip-tied his feet together so he couldn't move.

Earlier that evening, I'd left the garage door open and neglected to lock the door from the garage into the house because I thought I would be going out again to do more errands.

The intruders tossed Noah's cellphone into the microwave and cooked it. One guy shut Noah's computer and threw it in a manner where it bashed to the floor. They asked him how many people were upstairs. When he refused to say, they gagged him while one of the men held a gun to his head. The other two men ran upstairs and found me in my bedroom.

I shrieked in terror as I woke to see two men pointing guns at me. I jumped out of bed and tightened my robe. One of the gunmen was wearing medical scrubs and a surgeon's mask. He was short and stocky. The other guy was tall, wore dark sunglasses beneath a black knit hat that covered his thick black hair. He was wearing a dark leather jacket. For a split second, I thought this might be some kind of a sick prank, but I knew immediately that those guns were real. I felt as though I was leaving my body—completely numb. It was as if I was watching myself as a character in a scene from a scary movie.

The man wearing scrubs pulled off the surgical mask and shouted, "Where's the money? Where's the money?"

My children! They were the only things I was thinking about. Money?

"I don't have any money!" I said. "But, if you take me to the bank ATM, I'll give you everything in my account."

He kept yelling—sounds that made no sense to me.

I worried about looking at his face. I also worried that he was coming closer. I wondered why he was so angry. All I wanted was for them to take me away so that my children would not be harmed.

"Hold out your arms!"

I complied. He grabbed my arms and zip-tied them together in front. Then he slammed me into the nightstand and pushed me down on the floor. He stood over me pointing the gun to my head while the other guy ran down the hallway kicking doors to open them.

Raquel had heard me screaming and dialed 911. Then she locked her door and hid behind a dresser. Within seconds the tall person kicked the door in, saw her talking on her phone while crouched behind the dresser. He held the gun to her head.

"Give me the phone!"

As she did, she pointed to her bed and cried, "There's my wallet and tablet. Take them!" He'd looked at her cell phone and saw that she'd dialed 911. He ran out of Raquel's room and yelled, "Hey dude, we gotta split."

As the two men ran downstairs, I stood up and ran to the top of the staircase. I saw them head toward the door that led into the garage. I ran back to my room to get my cell phone and dialed 911.

A woman answered the call as I screamed, "Men just broke into my home. They had guns. Come quickly!"

Raquel came out of her room and we stared at each other. We were in shock as we then went downstairs. The dispatcher kept me on the phone. As Raquel and I rushed into the kitchen, Noah was still face down and squirming. Raquel grabbed a pair of scissors from the cabinet drawer and cut the zip-ties.

I checked the front door and saw it was locked, then raced to the door leading to the garage and locked it. "Where are the police?" I wailed to the dispatcher.

"They are there," she answered, "stay on the phone. They've surrounded your house."

Each second on the phone felt like hours. I couldn't stop shaking. Noah, Raquel, and I huddled in the foyer. The dispatcher spoke up again and said there was a police officer walking up the sidewalk to the front door. She told me to open the door and that we were now safe.

No! I didn't feel safe! What if those men were lurking? I wasn't sure I'd ever feel safe again for the rest of my life.

The officer introduced himself as a detective and asked if anyone was hurt. I shook my head. We were all still in shock and could hardly speak. My children clung to me as we listened to their directions. Another officer escorted us out of the house, and we walked barefoot on the icy sidewalk, shivering. He was escorting us to the home of neighbors, a young couple with two small children. She opened the door, ushered us into their kitchen, and gave us socks and blankets to warm us up. She found a pair of scissors and cut the zip-ties that were still on my wrists as she noticed scrapes and bruises. We couldn't see what was happening outside, but the officer explained that the police were taping the perimeter of my house, going through every inch of our house, taking fingerprints, and making sure that nobody was hiding.

After about 30 minutes had passed, the officer drove us to the police station. Two other detectives questioned us as I sat there hugging my children, crying, and thanking God that we were all alive. I couldn't even imagine how helpless Noah must have felt when the gunmen raced upstairs.

We answered their questions, but none of us could come up with any person so vicious as to hire gunmen to harm us. At some point, one of the detectives told us that this was a bizarre crime and we were all very lucky that no one was physically harmed. He said the odds were stacked against us because invaders who come equipped with guns and zip-ties are usually out to do damage, especially if they reveal their faces. He said that their crime is considered to be one notch below a murder and added how grateful he was that my daughter had the quick wits to dial 911.

Noah called Max, who was staying at his father's—my ex-husband's—home that night. Max said he would meet us at the house. Bobby, then my boyfriend, and now my husband, came to the station minutes after I called him. He hugged me and said that he couldn't believe what had happened. He had lived in this community for over 25 years, and crimes like this one had not ever occurred in his memory. He turned to Raquel and Noah and suggested that we all stay at his home for the night. The police asked him to leave and he went to get his home ready for us.

At 2:30 am, the police escorted Noah, Raquel, and me back to our home. Max was waiting for us by the front door. He hugged us and I cried once again. As we entered the house, I smelled burned metal and plastic—it was Noah's cell phone in the microwave. The police wanted to know if anything was taken, and after a few minutes of searching I said that my purse was gone. One of the officers told us that we need to return to the station the next afternoon for them to prepare facial composites of the criminals. All of us, including Max, needed to be fingerprinted. As the detectives were finishing their work, we gathered what we needed. Max drove us to Bobby's home where we all stayed that night.

Raquel and I shared a bedroom while Noah and Max slept in another room. Raquel told me that six months before, she'd dreamed about this exact scenario and said it was why she called for help within seconds. If not for that dream, she would have thought that I was doing one of my usual screams—as I do when I see a spider or some other insect—and she would have come into my room to remove it.

I didn't sleep for the rest of that night—or for many nights afterward.

In the morning, we all drove back to our home. A security company came to change all the locks, and the next day, a wireless alarm system was installed.

The alarm technician noticed that I was anxious and paranoid. I couldn't stay focused on his directions for setting up the alarm system. He gave me a free panic button to wear around my neck at home because he felt sorry for me. He explained that all I had to do was press and hold the button for two seconds and the police would come immediately.

When she saw it, Raquel said, "Mom, don't wear your fear."

I agreed with her but told her I would need some time to heal. She said that she would give me one week and I smiled for the first time since the home invasion.

CHAPTER 7

WHY?

Why would armed thugs want to invade my home? There was no money stashed there and I didn't work in a cash business or handle any cash transactions. Was it random? Maybe it was opportunistic. After all, the garage door was accidentally left open that night. But I knew that lots of the neighbors left garage doors open and doors unlocked—we felt we lived in a 'safe' place. Could I have been an intended target? Had I been followed as I went home from work that day?

Why?

These questions kept playing over and over in my mind, day after day.

The police informed me that they were going to surveil the house and neighborhood for the next few weeks. Staying home alone during those days and nights was not an option for me. I was terrified. After Noah and Raquel went back to college, friends came over to stay and keep me company. Bobby's dog, a Golden Retriever named Lucky, stayed with me during the days.

The panic button I'd been given was my safety net, yet it felt like an albatross around my neck—a constant reminder of the home invasion. Bobby and I took turns sleeping at each other's places. While he slept at my home, I'd lay awake listening to noises inside and outside. Muffled sounds scared me the most. I also followed the movement of lights on my bedroom ceiling and walls as cars drove by.

One night I noticed that the lights slowed down and then stopped in the middle of my ceiling. I jumped out of my bed and dashed to the window and looked below. I noticed a police car had just pulled into my driveway. It was just surveillance, but I still felt a rush of adrenaline.

When Bobby woke up and went to the bathroom at night, and I'd also wake, see his silhouette, and scream. My startle reflex had intensified; I was afraid of my own shadow and was extremely paranoid.

Noah and Raquel returned home from their college residences in May and new rules were implemented in our house. If they came home after 10 pm, they would call or text before they exited their car and came into the house. My thought was, "What if someone was waiting in the bushes ready to hurt them?" And the plan was that I'd have my cell phone handy and ready to call the police as they walked toward the front door.

Being in my car felt safer but I always checked my rearview and side mirrors to see if I was being followed. Lucky came with me for the car rides and after pulling out of my garage, I'd circle the block a couple of times, always on the lookout for strange cars parked in the neighborhood. I'd double check that the garage door was closed. When driving back home, I'd survey my neighborhood before I drove onto the driveway of my home.

My friends and family suggested that I move. My house no longer felt like a home. I put it up for sale and sold it within a few weeks. Bobby had asked me to move in with him and said, "I'll take care of you and your children. You will be safe with me in my house."

It was Bobby who helped me through one of the most horrific times in my life. I was so grateful to have someone who truly looked out for my children and me. He made me feel so very loved, something that I have never felt from a man before.

Yet…I was conflicted. As much as I appreciated his offer, I felt compelled to prove to myself that I was self-reliant and independent. I said to him, "I love you and I'd like to live with you one day…when I am strong and whole. For now, I need to focus on letting go of my fears."

I purchased a condominium in a nearby suburb and was scheduled to move into it a few months later. A new beginning and a safer environment were just what I needed. Even with the prospect of moving, my nerves were getting the best of me.

I couldn't help but think about the story of the day my father witnessed his mother and sisters being taken from his home and beaten to death by men he knew from his village. Though my home invasion was a minor experience compared to what he'd endured, I was now in a hyper-vigilant state of fear, just the way I'd know my dad to be all of my life. Was I following in his footsteps, destined to be paranoid and fearful forever? Was it ever going to be possible to let this go and move on?

It was Lea who I leaned on to help me get through this dark period of my life. During the course of psychological therapy, I noticed that my fear was morphing into rage and it fueled my body for quite some time. I kept thinking, "How dare those bastards come into my home, traumatize my children and scar us for life!" I wanted those thugs caught! I visualized them rotting away in jail!

Each week I contacted the detectives at the police station hoping for new information on my case. The fingerprints came back negative with just traces of my daughter's prints on her cell phone. Each day I checked the internet for the latest articles involving current arrests of home invaders in the Chicago metropolitan area and looked at hundreds of mugshots online. Those hoodlums were roaming the streets and preying upon other families. They had to be stopped and held accountable for their crimes.

As I was working with Lea, I discovered that anger had overshadowed my entire life. While anger is a natural human emotion which needs to be expressed, it can easily turn to rage and become unmanageable. Some people may quietly fume for days, months, and even lifetimes, but when triggered, they could explode. Others barely ever held back and spewed rage onto anyone and anything nearby. Expressing my anger was not something I readily did because I thought people would judge me for doing so. Unknowingly, I had repressed my anger for decades and alienated people who were confrontational and easily expressed their anger. They reminded me of my father who was erratic and mean. Lea said that I needed to take responsibility for my emotions; learn to feel them and let them go. Bottling up my anger and keeping it at a distance was not going to help me heal.

Fury is maddening. Like a hurricane, it can destroy anything in its path. When I was a child, my entire family suffered from my father's rage as he verbally, physically, emotionally, financially, and sexually abused various members. Unlike having an alcoholic parent and knowing when to escape from their insobriety, my father would become volatile at any given moment. I became vigilant, learned to be on guard, always ready to run and hide.

My father, Arie Kaplan, had survived unspeakable horrors during the Holocaust. Paralyzed with fear, he sought refuge in the forests of Eastern Europe where he miraculously survived for three-and-a-half years. He developed post-traumatic stress disorder and struggled with night terrors, flashbacks, paranoia, aggressive behavior, and rage.

I was scared of my father and compensated by striving to be the perfect daughter to gain his love and respect. He would pick up me and my siblings after school from the Jewish Community Center (JCC), and I'd be vigilant, waiting and watching for him. It was critical to be punctual. Once, my brother lost track of the time while he was in an art class. Furious, my father marched into the JCC and went directly to his class. He threw my brother on the floor and kicked him in front of the teacher and his friends. I made sure that kind of treatment would not ever happen to me.

As an adult, I finally realized that my father was damaged. He was incapable of loving himself, and therefore could not ever love me. I had to let go of any expectations that he'd ever take any interest in my life.

After my mom died, I saw him less frequently. Though I'd continue to invite him to my children's school assemblies, he always seemed too busy and said that he had other matters to take care of. That was perfectly fine with me. However, when his health was declining, he relied on me each week to drive him to his doctor appointments, the banks, and the grocery store. I became a dutiful daughter and helped him out.

But I did not love him.

Lea explained my father had been holding onto decades of anger. And I was following in his footsteps.

Fear stokes anger. I realized that I was not meant to live with this negativity and deserved peace and happiness.

Anger is an unhealed heart. When I forgave my dad on his deathbed, all the hatred I'd stored for him had dissipated, and a huge burden was lifted from me. I felt free. It was a long and difficult process but a rewarding outcome. I've come to realize that if one holds onto anger, then there's not much room left for joy and love.

Now I believe the home invasion may have been a test of my ability to forgive.

My father focused his entire life on revenge. He kept plotting the deaths of the men that murdered his family. What he never knew was that they were killed by members of the Polish resistance after World War II ended.

As I was working through my own trauma, I didn't know if those invaders were committing more crimes or serving a prison sentence, yet my hatred for them smothered my thoughts, controlled my feelings, and wasted my time and energy. Eventually, I decided that I was not going to worry about if and when they would be punished because it wasn't up to me. I didn't want to be consumed by what was going to happen to them and let the experience destroy my equilibrium. I could not control the wheels of justice, but I did learn to control my emotions and not let them get the best of me.

People who have bumped up against evil are often consumed by what should happen to the evildoers. My father was paralyzed in his quest for revenge and spent his entire life in a place of darkness. He never considered moving on. I was determined to create a new home for my family filled with laughter and joy. Lying in bed feeling hurt, persecuted, fearful or otherwise mistreated was not going to lead me to a better way of life. There was (and is) no glory in being a victim. Nor was it going to solve anything. Justice was not going to bring me peace of mind.

So, after 21 years of raising my three children in our home, I was eager to pack up that entire house and move. I wanted to create a new home for my family filled with laughter and joy. By December of that year, I had let the 'March madness' go away.

I chose to forgive those men.

I know now that even when bad things happen, I will have the fortitude to overcome the kind of pessimism and defeatism that plagued my father. Of course, I need to be careful. Yet I refuse to let myself be alarmed or paranoid. As the months passed after I forgave the criminals, my thoughts about the home invasion became less frequent and my startle reflex diminished.

Two-and-a-half years later, I received a call from the detective who had been assigned to my case. He asked me to come to the police station to look at some mugshots because he believed the FBI had caught the criminals. When I looked at the pictures, I immediately recognized the face of the man who'd held me hostage at gunpoint in my bedroom. He was the one who pulled down his mask, and I'd seen that he resembled another male friend of mine from years past. His mugshot made me certain it was him. It seemed to me that he'd gained some weight, and I saw a couple of musical notes tattooed on his cheek. I asked the detective if this man was short; I remembered towering over him. The detective acknowledged that his height was certainly below average.

The mugshot of the thug who wore sunglasses showed the same thick black hair, but I noticed he had a scary looking snake tattoo wrapped around his neck. The detective said he was the ringleader of a Filipino gang.

All three of those men, along with five other gang members, were currently serving a prison sentence in the state of Wisconsin. They had committed 15 home invasions in the states of Minnesota, Wisconsin, and Illinois. They were caught during an armed robbery at a fast food chain in Wisconsin.

The detective told me that the ringleader used a phone app to search for Asian families who owned cash-only businesses, most of which were restaurants. These men would monitor and study their victims for a week and follow them from their work to their homes, noting when the owner would bring home the cash. Then they'd force their way into each home and tie up all their victims. Some were physically harmed and in every home invasion, except for mine, they successfully stole tens of thousands of dollars. The detective explained that some Asian business owners were inclined to bring home cash rather than deposit it into the bank which made them more vulnerable to criminals. He also explained that home invaders wanted to face their victims—unlike burglars who do not want to be seen and prefer to break in during the morning or early afternoon when no one would be in the home.

I was stumped. My family does not look Asian, nor do I own a business. Even though my garage door was left open, these thugs took a huge risk by entering my home and exposing themselves without certainty there would be any cash on hand.

Why they chose my home still remained a mystery to the detectives who were on the case.

CHAPTER 8

AN ALIAS AND SOME ANCESTORS

When I was a teenager, my mother said my father used the alias Arie Kaplan, but he was born as Avrum Jankel Szteinsaper in Rajgròd, Poland. I was stunned to learn he'd kept an alias his entire life and wondered why he changed his name. My brothers and I were given Hebrew names after our relatives—of which most had perished in the Holocaust.

My family tree looks like this:

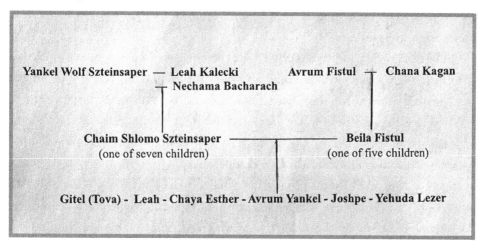

My great-grandfather Yankel Wolf Szteinsaper was born in 1840, and married Leah Kalecki. After Leah died, Yankel Wolf married Nechama Bacharach. Yankel Wolf had a total of seven children with both wives and among them was my grandfather, Chaim Shlomo, who was born in 1875. A few of my grandfather's siblings with their families left Poland long before World War II and settled all across the globe. I have met Szteinsaper relatives from Chile and Australia and connected with many others through Facebook. Most of the Szteinsaper clan remained in Poland and met their fate in 1942 as they were transported to Treblinka death camp and gassed to death. Only a handful of the Szteinsapers managed to survive.

Beila Fistul, the daughter of Avrum Fistul and Chana Kagan was born in 1896. Beila married my grandfather, Chaim Shlomo of Rajgròd, and they had six children. My father was their fourth child. Born in 1921, he was named after Beila's father, Avrum, and Chaim Shlomo's father, Yankel, who by the time of my father's birth had both passed away.

When the Nazis invaded Rajgròd on June 22, 1941, they demanded 100 Jews be brought to the center square where they were forced to strip down to their underwear then lined up in four-by-four rows on the main street. These Jews were forced to march down the main street while the Poles had to cheer from the sidelines. After walking a few miles away from the town into the forest, the Nazis executed all of them. The remaining Jews of Rajgròd were forced into a ghetto that was surrounded by barbed wire. Four months later, all of them were transported to Treblinka.

On June 22, 1941, under the authority of these Nazis, the two workers on Beila's farm forced their way into her home and savagely slaughtered her, Joshpe, Leah, and her baby. All because they had refused to be part of the public humiliation.

My aunt Chaya Esther and my great-grandmother Chana from Bialystok along with three of her children and their families were murdered at Treblinka. One of Beila's brothers was killed in Moscow in 1944.

In my family, my brother Howard was named after our grandfather, Chaim Shlomo. My brother Barry was named after grandmother Beila and aunt Joshpe. I was named after my two aunts, Chaya Esther and Leah. Naming a child after a deceased loved one is a tradition among Ashkenazi (European) Jews as a way to keep the memory of them alive and create a bond between the soul of the baby and the deceased relative. In Ashkenazi communities back then, many Jews were very superstitious and wouldn't allow naming a child after a living relative because they believed having the same name of living members in a family could confuse the Angel of Death when it came to take the soul of an elderly relative. God forbid it might accidentally take the child instead.

Because my mother never knew why my father had changed names, I asked my dad. He said, "During the war, I found an ID card with the name Arie Kaplan. I changed my name to save my life." Then he raised his index finger and pointed it directly at me, so that I would listen very carefully to him and said sternly, "Don't ever bring up this subject again! I don't want to talk about it." That was one of the last times I had discussed any of my father's personal experiences during the Holocaust.

Several decades later, I had an opportunity to ask my questions again.

I never thought much about the mystery behind my father's life until I started speaking to share stories from my first book. During the course of my talks, I would briefly discuss the lineage of the Szteinsaper family of Poland. When an audience member inquired about the family history of the real Arie Kaplan, I again wondered who was this man whose name I'd inherited?

My father was committed to tracing the Szteinsaper roots. He kept ancestral charts and correspondence records filed away; secured in a cabinet in his bedroom. My dad's master bedroom was his man cave, and he hardly ever allowed anyone from my family to enter, including my mother. For the first 16 years of my life, our family lived in a small, two-bedroom apartment in West Rogers Park, a Jewish neighborhood on the north side of Chicago. My mom and I shared the second bedroom and my older brothers slept in the den. It didn't occur to me that this was an abnormal arrangement until I was older and realized that parents usually sleep together in a master bedroom.

After I'd turned 16, our family moved into a larger, three-bedroom condominium in the area and continued living with the same bedroom set-up. At that time, I thought my father was extremely selfish, but my mother accepted his imperious home rules. My dad kept his bedroom closets, drawers, and desk neatly organized and could easily detect if someone were to rummage through his room.

On his desk there were always a half a dozen library books about the Holocaust, *The Sentinel*, a local, weekly Jewish magazine, and a book of the Torah. His desk drawers and file cabinets were always locked when he left home. He clasped the keys to a chain that attached to his belt.

My father warned me to never trust anyone because he never did. But he also did not trust my mother, brothers, or me. He always cautioned me to be suspicious of people who appear to be friendly. "They must want something from you," he'd said. But I noticed that my dad had a way of charming people, especially women, into getting what he wanted. When I took him to the doctor's office, he'd put on his friendly demeanor toward the female receptionist and nursing staff. He was determined to get free samples of medicine. When he didn't get what he asked for, he became angry and demanding.

My mother often said that my dad couldn't help himself; that he was living with the pain of his past, and that he'd survived the war by not trusting a soul. She also said "Karen, you don't have to agree with your father. Know that there are many kind and trustworthy people in the world." I could have easily been swayed by my father's perspectives, but thankfully, my mother taught me otherwise.

Back in the 1970s, my dad contacted the Mormon Church in Utah looking for ancestral information. The Mormons had traced and collected data from European families during the 1900s in order to find their ancestors and perform posthumous baptisms. My father ordered copies of microfilms which contained family records of births, deaths, and marriage contracts—along with land and town records from Rajgròd, Bialystok, and other villages throughout northeastern Poland.

Through this research, dad discovered that he'd come from a lineage of rabbis which made the process of tracing his roots that much easier. Our family ancestry dated back to the late 1400s when our ancestors were expelled from Spain during the Spanish Inquisition. The Szteinsapers had journeyed eastward through Europe and eventually settled in Poland. Jews began arriving in Rajgròd in 1587 and were hired by aristocratic landlords to collect rent and taxes from the peasants and to help maintain economic stability in the region.

By the late 17th century, the Jewish community there had erected a synagogue, *mikveh* (bath house), and built a cemetery. Jews became tailors, hatters, shoe-makers, farmers, fishermen, and carpenters; some owned shops where teas and alcohol products were sold. There was a Jewish food co-op where they bartered and sold fresh, organic farm-to-table foods.

Joshua Szteinsaper was the first of our family to emigrate to Rajgròd in the early 1700s and led the generations of Szteinsapers who flourished in northeastern Poland. Matchmakers were a highly respected profession back then and would arrange marriages between many of the villagers from the nearby communities. So, in 1913, Beila Fistul, at the age of 17, left her family in Bialystok, and married my grandfather, Chaim Shlomo who was 38 years old.

Growing up in Rajgròd, my father spoke Yiddish at home, Polish in public, and learned Hebrew in *cheder*, a Jewish school led by the town's rabbi. His oldest sister, Gitel, a Zionist pioneer who changed her name to Tova, left Poland in 1939, and emigrated to Palestine with a group of her peers. Yoshpe and Chaya Esther lived at home, while Leah—married with a baby—lived in Szczuczyn, a town nearby. My grandparents owned a house in the heart of Rajgròd, just off the town square, and a duck farm on the outskirts of town, two miles down the road.

My grandfather died in 1927 when my father was 6 years old. Soon after, his 2-year-old baby brother, Yehuda Leyzer, passed away. That is why grandmother Beila hired two local men to help manage the farm.

CHAPTER 9

MODERN UNION AND GEOGRAPHIC REUNION

In 2011, Bobby and I traveled to Poland so that I could learn more about my Jewish and Polish roots and visit my father's village. I wanted to see where dad was born and raised and possibly go inside his home. Bobby loves to travel and is always searching for fun and exotic places, but he never had Poland on his bucket list. Many Jews who travel to Poland visit the death camps, their family's villages, and the remnants of synagogues and Jewish cemeteries.

Because Bobby's parents were both Holocaust survivors and his father was transported to Auschwitz for a short period of time (only to be transferred to a labor camp), he felt compelled to see the death camp. His parents met and married in a Displaced Persons camp in Germany after the war. Unfortunately, most of his parents' relatives had been murdered during the Holocaust.

Bobby and I met in 2009 through a mutual acquaintance. I was attending a local restaurant opening when the photographer asked if he could take my picture and show it to his tall, single friend named Bob. He thought we would make a striking couple.

On our first date, Bobby openly shared stories about his father's experiences during the Holocaust, and we bonded over the tragic pasts of our families. Unlike my difficult childhood, Bobby grew up in a fairly normal household. His mother

Rae stayed home and took care of him and his siblings while his father worked several jobs. Bobby wished he could have spent more time with his dad but understood that he worked long hours to provide for the family.

Bobby took me to a Jackson Browne concert at the Ravinia Music Festival for our second date. When the show ended, we walked a few blocks back to his car while carrying our lawn chairs and empty food baskets. He had accidentally locked his car keys in the trunk and asked, "Have you ever been on a motorcycle?"

"Why?" I couldn't imagine where this conversation was going.

"Because we need a cab to take us back to my house. I'll pick up the spare car keys and then we'll ride back here on my motorcycle. You'll have to drive my car and follow me back home. Then I'll drive you back to your house."

"I've never been on a motorcycle." I felt apprehensive.

"No worries, I'm a very cautious rider," he said before he called for a cab.

When we arrived at his home, Bobby handed me his helmet and I placed it on my head. He securely fastened it and pulled down the face shield. Then he helped me put on his leather jacket. Bobby said, "You'll need to wear this to keep you warm. There's a cool chill in the air. Besides, you look pretty awesome."

I lifted up the face shield and said, "Promise me one thing, please don't tell my children I've been on a motorcycle. They'd kill me." I climbed onto the seat of the motorcycle and clung to him as we took off and gathered speed. I could tell he was smiling from ear to ear as I hugged him tightly.

After a couple of hours had passed, we'd solved the key problem and made our way back to my house. He parked in my driveway and asked, "Would you like to go out again?"

I answered with another question: "Does this sort of thing happen to you often?" I thought the situation was definitely a red flag that I was able to handle.

"Define, 'often.'" He smiled.

"Will you be picking me up in a car, cab, or motorcycle?" I asked and giggled.

We saw each other for the next 40 days in a row. During those days, we talked about opening up our hearts and taking risks in relationships. His wife died of breast cancer and he was ready to start dating again. I wasn't sure if I'd ever be ready after my divorce but being with him felt like home.

Bobby happens to be super laid back, meditates twice daily, and could be the poster child for patience. He also happens to be an animal and plant lover. He loved to let his dog Lucky and one of his two cats roam through the naturally landscaped garden he created in his backyard. Bobby's "go-to" place for a vacation had always been Negril, Jamaica. When there, he travels to a small and remote boutique hotel located on the limestone cliffs of the island, overlooking the inviting blue Caribbean Sea. He took me there several months after we started dating. We unpacked, stood on the balcony of our private cottage with a thatch-cut roof, and peered into the mesmerizing waters surrounded by tropical flowers, foliage, and hummingbirds. I said, "So what are we doing now?"

He looked at me in a strange way and said, "We're doing it."

"You're joking," I said with a laugh.

He was serious.

I said, "This place is magnificent, but I can't relax and do absolutely nothing for six days, I'll be bored."

Then I learned that he was trying to impress me and thought I would be happy in his paradise. He didn't realize that I'd be missing the urban landscape, the bright city lights, traffic noise and the sounds of people talking. It's the hustle and bustle of city life that stimulates my inner self.

Each day during that trip to Jamaica, I'd sing a line from the "Green Acres" TV show's theme about how I loved him, but "give me Michigan Avenue."

Over the years, I've noticed that Bobby has distinctive mannerisms that do not match up with other Jewish kids who were raised in West Rogers Park. When he drinks a beverage, he extends his pinky as if he was part of the British elite. When we walk together, he folds his arm to his chest leaving me room for me to insert my arm, the way a European man would escort a lady in the long-ago centuries. He'd mentioned once that he loves tophats and I actually bought him a Victorian black hat for his birthday. When he greets someone for the first time, he extends his hand and slightly bows his head. His food choices are interesting, too. He will eat anything with peas, an English food favorite. I finally told him that he must have been an English gentleman in a recent past life, and it made him laugh.

Bobby's mom Rae would light up with the biggest smile whenever she'd see him. It seemed that her son could do no wrong. She once told me that when Bobby was younger, he would protect his family and friends from bullies. One day while walking with his little cousin to school, a bully rode up on a bicycle and harassed his cousin. By the end of the day, the principal had called Rae into his office and told her that Bobby took a boy's bike and hid it. Rae told the principal that whatever Bobby did, it must have been for a good reason.

Bobby and I had been dating a few years when his mom, then 89 years old asked me, "Karen, when will you marry my son?"

I told her that I wasn't sure if I would ever get married.

From the look on her face, I realized I never should have been so forthcoming. She was disappointed. That same day, Rae advised Bobby to start dating other women.

By age 91, Rae rejoiced at our wedding. She passed away a few months later, knowing that her son was in love and had a wife at his side.

My mother would have loved Bobby had she lived to meet him. As for my father....

One Saturday in October 2009, my father walked from his girlfriend Bella's apartment to his psychiatrist's office in Uptown Chicago for his regular checkup. The doctor's staff wanted to make sure that my father had a ride home and would not let him leave the office. My father had difficulty understanding them because of his hearing loss. He'd become agitated. Instead of trying to communicate to him in writing, slowing their speech, or calling me, the receptionist reported a serious problem and the psychiatrist sent him to the hospital psychiatric ward against his will.

That same Saturday night, Bobby had I had planned a dinner date. Dressed and ready to head out, I received a call from my father. He seemed nervous and irate. I told Bobby that our plans had to change and asked him if he could accompany me to meet my father in the psych ward so that I could release him.

We drove into the city to the hospital and waited for my father in a tiny corner room on the psych ward. I sat at a small table and Bobby sat behind me against the wall. Soon my father appeared, dressed in a hospital gown covered by his worn-out sweater along with hospital slippers. The staff had taken his dentures and the rest of his clothing. He was terrified and upset. He sat down at the table and glared at

Bobby. Instead of demanding to be freed immediately, I knew my father was going to focus on Bobby. He asked me in Yiddish, "Who is that man sitting behind you?"

I replied loudly in English, "He is my boyfriend." I turned my head to look at Bobby and he appeared nervous.

"Is he Jewish?" my father asked.

"Yes," I answered, "he is a child of Holocaust survivors."

"Good, now get me out of this *meshugoyim haus* [insane asylum]," he yelled.

He was there for a week until I was able to have him released. Traumatized from this experience, my father called me each day terribly upset that they refused to return his teeth and personal belongings.

This experience in the hospital was the exact nightmare he'd always dreaded and anticipated. The fear of being taken away.

And that was the first and only time Bobby saw my dad.

When Bobby and I were in Kraków and Warsaw in 2011, we visited the old Jewish quarters, Holocaust memorials, and ghetto areas. We spent an emotional day at Auschwitz, one of the largest mass murder sites in the world. Then we hired a tour guide named Maciej to drive us to Bialystok and Rajgròd.

In Bialystok, I discovered some additional records from my grandmother Beila's family. Beila's father Avrum died while she was young. Her mother Chana moved the family from Janowo, a small village, to Bialystok to start a new life. I visited the original apartment building where Beila once lived. This large white structure had miraculously survived the Nazi bombings and was in the midst of renovations. While strolling through my grandmother's once flourishing Jewish neighborhood, we learned that more than half of the population of this town was Jewish before World War II.

Maciej led us to a memorial dedicated to Jews who perished in the Great Synagogue of Bialystok. Built in 1913, this grand edifice had hosted prestigious cantors from all over Europe and celebrated national Polish holidays with local and national elected officials. The synagogue was destroyed when the Nazis barricaded approximately 2,000 Jews who where residents of Bialystok inside the building and set it on fire. All that remains is the large, twisted, black metal frame from the dome of the synagogue, resting in an awkward position on the ground.

The Great Synagogue of Bialystok.

Each morning at the hotel where we stayed in Bialystok, we indulged in a lavish Polish buffet breakfast which included pierogis, sauerkraut, stuffed cabbage, rye bread, bialys, and all sorts of smoked fish. I remembered that my mom would often make some of these dishes for my dad. He loved her cooking, but I never heard him thank her. My dad would often stop at the neighborhood Jewish deli on Devon Avenue and pick up a dozen bialys topped with sautéed onions and poppy seed filling. I remembered how he'd enjoy those semi-flat, savory rolls, especially if they had just come out from the oven.

From Bialystok, we drove 45 minutes north to arrive in my father's hometown. Rajgròd today is a small, remote fishing and boating village nestled on picturesque Lake Rajgròdzkie. Bobby took out his camera and video recorder and filmed the area. We walked along the peninsula shore and saw cranes, swans, and wild ducks swimming on serene blue waters. Local fishermen were catching pike, perch, and whiting. I couldn't help but think that my grandmother Beila must have made some of the tastiest homemade gefilte fish back then.

I noticed red marshes and lush green vegetation bordering the shoreline as ancient primeval forests created a stunning backdrop to the lake and village. The dense woods were filled with pine trees and Norwegian spruce. Eagles,

Fishermen on Lake Rajgròdzkie before WWII.

Lake Rajgròdzkie and the Catholic Church in the background.

The wooden synagogue (building on the far left) by Lake
Rajgròdzskie. Behind the synagogue is Castle Hill.

woodpeckers, owls, and other birds nest were nesting. While staring into this vast
forest, my stomach dropped, and I felt a sense of dread. I said to Bobby, "I can't
imagine how my father survived three-and-a-half years hunted by the Nazis, being
preyed upon by wolves and other wild animals that roam these lands."

"As enchanted as these forests appear today," Bobby replied, "they were death
traps for so many Jews."

Perched above the rooftops in the town, on the telephone poles, and on special
towers are nests made by storks. I observed with awe as these tall, long-necked,
white birds with massive wingspans flew through the countryside to bring back
food for their fledglings.

We noticed a steep hill overlooking the lake where a fortified citadel once stood
centuries ago. Surely, this *shtetl* must have been Gan Eden (the Garden of Eden) for the
Jewish community for several centuries. In fact, Rajgròd means 'the city of paradise.'

We strolled along the main road in Rajgròd—it's called Warsaw Street and it
is roughly five city blocks long—to Rajgròdski market, in the town's square. The

square has a triangle-shaped grass park with an old drinking fountain, a small, pale green water pump, a flagpole, and a shabby old bulletin board with no information on it. Lining the streets are faded brown and gray homes, as well as beige and white, two-story tenement houses that were built at the beginning of the 20th century. Some of the structures were painted over with inharmonious colors, such as chartreuse, bright orange, and lime yellow. A few small stores in town have signs selling *lody* (ice-cream) and the Zywiec brand of beer. At the edge of the town stands a neo-gothic style, red brick church. It looms over every building on site.

Rajgròd's bus station, a small, one-story, mustard yellow shack, faces the town square. Adjacent to the station is a two-story house with a bright pink facade and gray cement sides located at the corner of Maya and Placa 1000 Lecia Streets. This was my father's childhood home for 19 years of his life—until that fateful day when the Nazis marched into Rajgròd.

When I first laid eyes on my father's house from across Rajgròdski market, I froze. My heart was pounding. Seventy years had passed, and time was moving forward, yet as I stared at his home, it seemed as though time stood still.

In this surreal moment, everything around me faded into the background except for this pink home. My imagination took me on a tour. In my mind's eye, I saw myself crossing the road, slowly walking up the front steps, and opening the wooden door. Attached to the door frame was a small silver *mezuzah*. I touched it. A *mezuzah* is a symbol that reminds those that live in the house of their connection to God and their Jewish heritage. I stepped inside and heard sounds emanating from another room. I followed the noise as I imagined walking down the hallway. Standing at the kitchen entrance, I 'saw' my grandmother Beila. She was using an old wooden ladle to stir a large pot of steaming sweet and sour borscht. My father, then a young boy, and his older sisters, were seated at the table. They were chattering and impatiently waiting for Beila to serve the meal. Then I saw as Beila served her children their dinner, and I watched my father slurp down the soup and ask for more.

Next, my dreamscape changed to nighttime and the house turned dark and quiet. I walked up the stairs to my father's bedroom and watched him sleeping soundly. He looked so sweet and innocent. What was he dreaming about—what he wanted to be when he grew up?

Lake Rajgròdzkie today with Castle Hill in the background.

Then I wandered downstairs and saw my grandmother nodding off in a rocking chair near the fireplace. On a mantel nearby was a Hanukkah menorah and a pair of silver candlesticks used for the sabbath.

This dreamlike scene ended when Bobby said, "Karen, let's head to your father's home and see if someone might be there to let us in."

Maciej led us across the street and knocked on the door. No one answered, so we circled around to the fenced backyard adjacent to the bus station. In the yard was an old wooden shack with the door slightly ajar. A little German Shepard pup was happily wagging its tail and running toward us. It seemed that there was someone in the shed. I wondered if that shed might have been my father's hiding place where he'd watched his home be invaded.

Maciej kept on calling out, asking if anyone was in there. After several minutes, a woman who appeared to be in her 60s exited the shed. She picked up the dog and was noticeably uninterested in talking to us. Maciej explained, "We just arrived into town. This woman standing next to me is the granddaughter of Beila Szteinsaper, the woman who lived in this home before the war. Her father was born and raised in this house and recently passed away. She traveled all the way from America and would be grateful to spend a few minutes inside this home. She would like to say a prayer for her family that died during the war."

The woman, still holding her dog tightly, said, "Yes, the Szteinsapers were the previous owners but my mother had legally purchased the property a few years after the war had ended. When she died, I became the rightful owner of the house," then she added, "this woman can say a prayer where she is standing because the Szteinsapers owned the bus lot, too."

The Polish woman turned away and walked inside the home through the back door. Extremely disappointed, I had no choice but to say a prayer where I was standing. I did not blame her for not letting me into her house. If three strangers came knocking at my door as we had, I would have done the same thing. I wouldn't let them in.

Maciej walked away to give me some personal space. Bobby continued to film from a distance. I felt compelled to recite out loud the *Kaddish,* a mourner's prayer for my grandmother Beila, my aunts Yoshpe, Chaya Esther, Leah and her family, and all the murdered Jews of Rajgròd. I wanted all these souls to know that they had not been forgotten. As I spoke the Hebrew words, my voice cracked and tears

Rajgròd's yellow bus station. To its left, the pink house
was Avrum Szteinsaper's childhood home.

were streaming down my cheeks. Then the moaning and wailing began. I stood
there, hunched over, and buried my face in my palms. Raw emotions consumed me
as I attempted to recite each and every word. I mourned the loss of ever knowing
my family. I grieved for all the Jews of Rajgròd, and especially for my father, whose
world had been shattered.

After my first visit to Rajgròd with Bobby, I was determined to build a monument in memory of my family and for all the Jews who'd perished in Rajgròd.
This memorial would be a place of prayer for all those who wished to acknowledge
their ancestors. The Jews who'd inhabited this village in that era would not ever
be forgotten.

My Israeli cousin Avi (Tova's son) and I, together with a newly created committee of descendants of Rajgròd, worked for three years to raise funds for the
memorial project. Avi hired an Israeli sculptor, and by September of 2014, a

Rajgròd Memorial, at the unveiling.

ceremony took place at the site of the abandoned Jewish cemetery of Rajgròd. For over 70 years the desolate graveyard was unkempt; hidden with an overgrowth of trees from the surrounding forests. Small fragments of tombstones were spread throughout the area, and a few dug up graves were noticeable. The land there is estimated to hold 2,000 to 3,000 graves.

When the memorial was unveiled, two pristine white stone sculptures stood proudly side-by-side against the backdrop of the wooded cemetery. The rectangular block has the Star of David intersected by a break, a crack, in the stone. This is symbolic of the broken Jewish life and the end of the Jewish community of Rajgròd. The opening of the Jewish star gives a glimpse of this past, a recollection that Jews once coexisted with their Christian Polish neighbors. On the adjacent monument words are inscribed in Hebrew, Polish, and English: "The Rajgròd Jewish cemetery was founded in the 18th century and was destroyed during WWII."

Just a few months after the unveiling, I learned that the memorial was vandalized. A perpetrator took a jackhammer and drilled into the center of the star,

Rajgròd Memorial, after the vandalism.

destroying it. It felt like someone jabbed me in the chest and ripped out my heart. Shock came first, and then feelings of anger and sadness prevailed.

My heart was bleeding.

Weeks later, our committee decided to have a local sculptor carve a larger Jewish star onto the monument.

In May of 2015, I returned to Rajgròd with two of my children, Max and Raquel. We met with the mayor and town council. I presented my memoir, *Descendants of Rajgròd: Learning To Forgive*, and then we discussed ways to prevent any further vandalism to our beloved monument. The mayor explained that the property of the cemetery was under the jurisdiction of the forest authority, not the township of Rajgròd, but he encouraged those who manage it to install cameras high up in

Vandalized once again.

the trees. This outer area of Rajgròd is desolate, has minimal traffic, and by now, I felt it was not an ideal location to erect the monument.

The memorial today.

Yet desecration struck once again. A few months later, a 16-year-old juvenile delinquent was caught on camera spray painting the memorial in red. The Polish slogans he'd written said something like, "Go back to the gas chambers," and, "Whores." The police arrested the teen and the mayor had his staff attempted to remove the vile graffiti.

Again, I felt violated. Our once magnificent memorial looked like it had been through war. And yet this antisemitic occurrence seemed to have mimicked the way of life of the Jews of Rajgròd.

On that trip, I led Max and Raquel through their grandfather's village, again I saw his home from the outside, and we visited the cemetery and lake. Then we drove to Treblinka, the extermination camp, where most of my father's family were transported and murdered alongside 800,000 Jews.

During my two visits to Rajgròd, I happened upon Krystyna, a petite yet robust old woman who was 14 years old during the Nazi invasion. Around the corner from my father's home, a half-mile down a dirt road, toward the lake was her house—and it looked to be well over 100 years old. The gray, warped wood panels covering the sides and roof were buckling and I thought one nasty storm would completely demolish the place. Both times Krystyna was outside of the home, feeding dozens of her free-range chickens. Nearby stood a dilapidated barn which housed her prized possessions, six dairy cows and seven pigs.

Krystyna's face was aged with deep wrinkles, and gray hair was visible at the edge of her hairline—underneath her *babushka*. It took her a few minutes to recognize me and she asked the tour guide, while staring at me, "Last time you were here, you were much fatter. Did you lose weight?"

Max and Raquel at Treblinka.

I wasn't sure if she was complimenting me, but I said, "*Tak, tak* and thank you." Krystyna had a warm smile though I saw her two front teeth were missing. She warmed up to my interpreters each time and invited us into her home. She was the most gracious host as she served us tea and kept us warm as she shoveled black chunks of coal into a cast iron stove.

"I remember your grandmother," she said. "We called her by her nickname, Kachorka, meaning 'duck.' She was a very tall and beautiful woman. She lived in the center of town near Maya Street, right next to the bus station. There was a store next to her home, and she may have owned it. I would go to the store and buy food. We chatted all the time. She was friendly. Many people in town would shop at the store, and we would all talk to one another," Krystyna reminisced.

What a blessing it was to have met Krystyna and listen to her share fond memories of my grandmother, Beila. She also spoke about the relationship she herself had with her other Jewish neighbors. "Even though the Jews and Christians lived in separate neighborhoods, there was a community and we mostly all got along. I went to school with the Jewish children. My friend Bloomka, was in my class at school and we would play childhood games together. Her parents would come to buy milk from our farm. Bloomka and I had another friend named Chaim, and he would eat our sausage and didn't care that we mixed meat with milk. Once when I was at his home, I remember eating matzoh. In the wintertime, the three of us would go sleigh riding down Castle Hill by the lake." These memories made her smile as she spoke.

Her demeanor changed when she began to talk about the war.

"The Russians first invaded Rajgròd in April 1940. They vandalized the town church, killed the Catholic priest and 60 Christian Poles, including my brother. Many of the Christians were sent to the work camps in Siberia and a few returned after the war. Some of the Jews were sent to fight on the Russian front." Krystyna's tone was sober.

I knew that being sent to fight on the Russian front meant immediate death for the Jews. "Can you tell me about the Nazi incursion?"

"The Russians were forced to retreat when the Nazis seized Rajgròd in June 1941. They set up a ghetto fence of barbed wire near your grandmother's home. Some Polish neighbors were trying to hide a few Jews, and they all were killed. The Jews, the sick, and the old Polish people—along with the Romani people—were taken to the ghetto. Then eventually they sent them away, but I don't know where they were taken," she said.

"What happened to all the Jewish structures?" I asked.

From her kitchen window she pointed to the lake and said, "Over there is Castle Hill, where there was once a synagogue and school. The town would gather on the hill and have special ceremonies. The *mikveh* was near the lake and there was another synagogue next to it. A couple miles down the road near your grandmother's farm is an abandoned Jewish cemetery. The Germans removed most of the headstones so they could pave roads. Everything was destroyed."

My ancestors, the Szteinsapers, sought safety and made Rajgròd, Poland their homeland for over 200 years. During that time, they developed a rich religious, social, and cultural way of life—never succumbing to the turmoil of foreign rulers and intermittent antisemitism. But this city of paradise turned into sheer hell for my family and the Jewish community when the Nazis invaded.

Krystyna and Karen during her second visit to Rajgròd.

As I walked through the streets of modern Rajgròd during those two trips it was hard to imagine that Jewish life had ever existed here. It was comforting to listen to Krystyna's fond memories of my grandmother and her Jewish friends from decades long ago. Learning about my family heritage and understanding my ancestors' way of life helped me appreciate all their struggles and provided me with a sense of grounding.

Yet, I had a yearning to uncover the mystery of a man named Arie Kaplan, a complete stranger. His surname will forever be ensconced in my being and will be carried on for many generations to come. After reviewing hundreds of my father's files after his death and searching for documentation about the man whose identity my father had assumed, I came away empty handed. The nagging questions persisted. What did my father mean when he said that his identification saved his life? Who was this man? Did my father know Arie Kaplan before or during the war? How did he obtain his identification card, and could this man be alive today? Why was my dad so secretive? Was it his long-standing paranoia?

"I must continue this search," I thought.

CHAPTER 10

THE ONLY EVIDENCE

ℵ

How I wished I'd learned about my father's life during the Holocaust. Very few survivors were willing to share their experiences with their children. My brother Howard was my father's main confidant. Dad thoroughly enjoyed discussing Jewish history, religion, politics, and the Holocaust with him. I was never included in any of these conversations. At that time, I was young, and frankly not all that interested. As I matured, my father would have never considered discussing his war experiences with me because I was a girl. It was only through random comments that I'd learned bits and pieces of my father's past.

One cold winter morning before I left the house for school, my father and I were waiting in the car for my brothers. I was shivering, my nose was turning red, and I could see my breath as fog. I asked dad if he would start the engine and turn on the heat.

"Stop *kvetching*!" he said, his voice stern. "You don't know the meaning of cold weather. I survived frigid winters in the forests of Poland by sleeping on a bed of snow."

From that point on I never again complained to my father. It was useless. I also never grumbled much about anything. I'd grown up hearing stories about the starving people in China and I was grateful that my family and I had a roof over our heads and food on our plates. That perspective has stayed with me to this very day and it's often hard to listen to people complain about trivial matters. When I'd hear about how a friend missed a manicure appointment or a maid did not show up for the day, it meant nothing to me.

By the time Howard became a bar mitzvah, he had surpassed my father in height and weight and was physically stronger than him. Around that same time, Howard had witnessed my father beating my mom. He went into action and put our dad in a headlock then screamed at my dad to never hit our mother again or else he'd kill him.

After that incident, our father seemed to gain respect for Howard and he never laid a hand on my mom from that point on—as far as I know. I was a scared little girl but felt safe having my big brother around to protect us from our dad.

Howard was ordained as an orthodox rabbi and eventually acquired a pulpit as the head rabbi in a synagogue in Cliffside Park, New Jersey. Each week he sent our family his typed sermon in the mail because we were his biggest admirers. Standing at six-foot-six, Howard had a wide arm span and gave very gentle hugs. When he officiated at my first wedding, he was so nervous standing in front of 275 guests that he forgot to tell my husband to kiss me at the appropriate time at the end of the ceremony.

I think it was an omen.

During that wedding, Howard reinforced the importance of having children and repopulating the six million Jews that perished in the Holocaust. My father was impressed as he watched Howard officiate. My mother was filled with *nachas*, a Yiddish term that describes how her heart was swelling with pride as she listened to Howard speak and how he adoringly looked at me under the *chuppah*. Though that marriage ended after 17 years, it was a cherished moment for my entire family.

At the age of 35, Howard was married with two young children living his dream being a rabbi. He told me once that he wanted to honor our family's heritage by continuing the lineage of rabbis. He took a second job selling life insurance to earn enough money to send his children to private Jewish schools. My brothers and I went to school on scholarships and it made Howard feel like a second-class student. He vowed to never accept charity. A hard worker, Howard was so full of life.

We were shocked the night he died in his sleep.

As a result, my father's rage intensified. My mother went into an even deeper depression. My brother Barry and I were in disbelief. It took me a long time to recover from Howard's death. I tried to be there for my mom by bringing my children to visit as much as possible. She was suffering; my children brought her joy and gave her moments of relief.

One of my greatest regrets is that Howard and I never discussed any of the conversations he'd had with our father about Rajgròd.

When my son Noah was in high school, he interviewed and videotaped my father about his life in the Holocaust for a history project. At that time, my father was 87 years old and his paranoia had worsened. It surprised me when he agreed to help with Noah and talk about his family and life in Rajgròd before the war. When Noah asked him how his family was killed, my father broke down and wept.

It was the first time I'd heard that story.

Seeing him crying was difficult. I felt helpless, but I couldn't hug him. I knew he'd not let me. The only other time I'd seen him in such despair was at Howard's funeral. He wailed with such intensity that I had to hold him upright because I thought he was going to fall into Howard's grave.

The simplicity of Noah talking with my father about his past was an astonishing feat because I was always afraid to bring up the subject. Questions of my father's alias as Arie Kaplan were not mentioned during this interview, so the mystery was buried along with my father when he died two years later in 2010.

My father's nephew, Avi Tzur was the second son of Tova and the only other family member with whom my dad had shared information about Rajgròd. Avi is the quintessential *sabra* [a native-born Israeli]. Born in 1950, two years after the birth of the state of Israel; he was raised in Rishon LeTzion, a town situated east of Tel Aviv. I know him to be confident, bold, and fearless—the very symbol of the modern-day Israeli Jew. He served in the Israel Defense Forces (IDF) as a captain in the Yom Kippur War.

My father had discussed returning to Rajgròd with Howard. After Howard died, my father asked Barry to travel with him, but that trip never happened. When Avi decided to travel to Rajgròd in 1990, my father wanted to join him on his trip. I called Avi in Israel months before I left for my first visit to Rajgròd and asked him, "Why didn't my father meet you in Poland?"

Avi said, "Before I left for Poland, your father wanted me to obtain a personal letter from Lech Walesa, the president of Poland, that would ensure his safety there. Underneath his tough exterior he was a frightened man."

"What did you tell him?"

"It was inconceivable to get a letter from the government. Maybe that's why he never went. But he drafted a map of the town, the location of his home, their farmhouse, the synagogues, *mikveh* and Jewish cemetery. He also gave me the names of the two killers who took part in murdering our grandmother and aunts."

"Did your mother provide you with any details of Rajgròd?" I asked.

"No, my mother as well as my father refused to discuss their past with me. They were emotionally distant."

"Why do you think your parents did not express any interest? Why were you interested in going to Poland?"

"I strongly believe in connecting to my roots. I wanted to see where my parents were born. They both wanted to disconnect from the old cultural background of the Eastern Europe Jew. My parents' generation desired a new Jewish character. Personally, I believe this was an excuse because it was too difficult dealing with all their losses. They carried a lot of guilt, but there is no judgement."

Avi then relayed a story about how his parents met before the war. He said, "My mother, Tova, was best friends with a girl who was dating my father, Chaim. All three were planning to go to Palestine in 1939 with a group of other Jewish pioneers, but this girl needed to remain in Poland to take care of her ailing mother. Tova and Chaim left for Palestine without her and she died in the Holocaust with her mother. My parents carried plenty of guilt that lasted throughout their lives. Guilt for leaving their friend, guilt for leaving their families, guilt for marrying each other, and guilt for surviving."

I thought about how living with survivor's guilt is quite debilitating, and it obviously had left scars on Avi and his older brother. The next generation was clearly impacted by those who survived.

Avi added, "When I left for Poland, all I had was your father's drawing of the *shtetl*. He had an extraordinary memory of the layout of the town. The map was very accurate except that he was off by a 90-degree angle. Once I figured that out, I was able to locate our grandparents' house and the abandoned Jewish cemetery."

"Did my father ever discuss why he changed his last name to Kaplan?"

"No, he never did. But your father had one request for me when I returned to Poland. Since I was a soldier in the Israeli Defense Force, he wanted me to hunt down the men that killed the Szteinsapers and kill them. I figured he was still afraid that they might be looking for him. Maybe that is why he never changed his name back to Szteinsaper. I told your dad that I wasn't going to Poland to kill anyone but that I would try to go inside the Szteinsaper home and find any relics that may have belonged to our family."

When Avi traveled to Rajgròd, he too was unable to enter our grandparents' home. But he was glad to have seen the village where his mother had lived.

Without any more family direction, I began my research at The Wilmette Family History Center of the Church of Jesus Christ of Latter-day Saints that is connected to the Salt Lake City's Mormon Library. After spending a week working with the staff, I came up empty-handed.

The Statue of Liberty-Ellis Island Foundation site has a passenger record of a 24-year-old male named Arie Kaplan who entered Ellis Island February 2, 1950, on a ship called USS General A.W. Greeley. The ship embarked from the port of Bremerhaven, Germany on January 19, 1950 and carried mostly Eastern European refugees. My father was also a passenger.

Arie Kaplan is a Jewish name. The surname Kaplan is common among European Jews especially in Germany, Poland, and Hungary. The name Kaplan indicates esteemed priestly lineage, a descendant of the sons of Aaron (brother of Moses), who were the priests or *kohanim*, serving in the Holy Temple of Jerusalem. JewishGen.org, a website for Jewish genealogy, and The United States Holocaust Memorial Museum archives list several Kaplans. A few were

Ship's manifest showing the name of Arie Kaplan.

USS General A.W. Greeley.

named Arie Kaplan, but I found none who were within the same age range as my father.

Six months passed. I had not gained any information about the stranger named Arie Kaplan. I was frustrated and ready to give up. Feeling defeated, I called Lea hoping she might have a suggestion where I could do more research.

Lea's responses are sometimes out of left field (or should I say the etheric field?) and they take me completely off my guard. For example, soon after the home invasion, she came to my house with her collection of healing rocks, a selenite dagger, and a kali wand. She walked all throughout the home, especially into the rooms where the criminals entered, and cleared their energies. But she also reminded me to clear myself from this harrowing experience because the fear, anger, and paranoia were paralyzing my mind and body.

In response to my call about Arie Kaplan, Lea said, "Why don't we bring forth the spirit of this man?

"Seriously? You can do that? It never occurred to me that you can conjure up a spirit that I've never met. How crazy is that?"

During earlier therapy sessions with Lea, the spirit of my mother and Howard had appeared a few times. My mom's spirit, on occasion, had imparted her opinion on some difficult family issues. Mothers will always be mothers, even in spirit. While growing up, I often heeded my mother's advice. She'd encouraged me to marry a physician, or any professional who would financially provide for me and my future children. While studying at the University of Illinois in nutrition and medical dietetics, I met my first husband, a Jewish doctor, and married him once I graduated. No one in my family was surprised. But when I divorced him everyone was shocked.

When my mom graduated from high school her goal was to find a husband. She felt like an old maid when she married my dad—and she was only 19 years old. Her girlfriends had already been married for two years and had started families.

My mother was a battered woman with low self-esteem and believed that it was far better to be with someone who is harmful than to live alone. My views were and still are quite different. I vowed not to repeat her life and would rather live by myself than in a relationship that lacked praise, warmth, and affection.

Looking at early pictures of my mom, I noticed a sparkle emanating from her big brown eyes, and her sweet, endearing smile. She was the ultimate *balabusta*, a Yiddish term for homemaker. She single-handedly raised my brothers and me because my father was hardly ever around. He'd never help with any household chores but expected a hot meal every night as soon as he came home. Later on, when my brothers and I were in grade school, my mother was employed at Von Steuben High School as a teacher's aide and worked her way up to become assistant to the vice-principal. For many years she'd handed my father her payroll checks and in return he gave her a strict allowance for groceries and gas. But in her late 50s she finally stood up to him and demanded that she keep her money. I was so proud of her.

Food was an expression of her love, and mom enjoyed cooking and feeding her children and grandchildren. Max, Noah, and Raquel always looked forward to weekends when she would come over and bring homemade sweet and sour meatballs and kugel. Her chocolate chip and walnut mandelbread was my absolute favorite, and I continue to bake this for special occasions and holidays.

My mom and I would talk frequently throughout the day and she could never go to bed until she knew I was home safe at night. She was a worrier. When I was on my honeymoon, my mom called my mother-in-law and asked if she had heard from my husband and me. My mother-in-law said that we might be hiking somewhere in the mountains and there was no way to communicate with us. My mom panicked and couldn't relax until we returned home eight days later. I think I inherited that gene from my mom because I constantly over-worry about my children's safety and happiness, but I don't let on as much as I think I do. My daughter knows not to tell me that she is going out for the evening, because if I don't hear from her, I call, text, and Facebook her friends until someone tells me that she is fine.

Over the years as my father's behavior was spiraling downwards, my mom continued to tolerate the abuse as her love of food turned into an addiction. She became morbidly obese. The brightness that once shined within her had faded away.

"Mom, divorce him already," I'd say. "Come live with me. We have room in the house for you."

"I don't want to impose on you, your husband, or your children," she said, and reminded me that my father had been through a catastrophic past, he couldn't help himself, and that he would never agree to a divorce. I was frustrated with her because she had a job, a car, and money in her account. She didn't need my father to provide for her anymore and she didn't have to worry about taking care of her children. She had no more valid excuses. But she continued to cook hot meals for him, wash his clothes, and clean the house. Her loyalty to my dad was like Stockholm syndrome, a survival mechanism where the victim sympathizes with the abuser. Living with my father was hellish, but my mother deserved to be happy. I wished I could have done more to help her, like putting down a deposit on a rental property so that she could move close to me. She would have never agreed.

My mom spent the last six weeks of her life in the hospital. During that time, I would bring my three little ones to visit with her. They made cards and drew pictures that we taped on her hospital bedroom walls. Max would sing, "Lean on Me," a song which he learned that summer at day camp. He was 9-years-old at that time. To this day, whenever I hear the song, I think of my mom and hope she is sending me hugs and kisses from her resting place. I loved her with all my heart and when she died my world fell apart.

Now, several years after my mother had passed, I asked Lea, "How will this spirit of Arie Kaplan know to come forward? How will I know it is truly him? Does he even speak English?"

"Karen, all these years of channeling, I've been able to communicate with many spirits that have crossed over who come from varied cultures and speak different languages. I can hear their thought forms in English, though I cannot always pronounce foreign names or get the exact spellings. So, let's give this a try and see if he comes through."

My conventional ways of researching Arie Kaplan had failed, so I had nothing to lose meeting him through a psychic channeler. Lea and I scheduled a morning meeting at my home on March 12th, 2016. At that time, she was planning travel to Illinois from southern Florida for a family celebration. She'd made the Sunshine State her home to avoid the chilling winters in the Midwest.

CHAPTER 11

GOOSEBUMPS

I had tossed and turned all night long, not knowing what to expect from my session with Lea that was to take place the next morning. My stomach was twisted in knots and my head spun with all sorts of hypothetical situations about this stranger named Arie Kaplan and his connection with my dad. Was it possible that this man knew my father before the war? Could they have been neighbors in Rajgròd, classmates, or friends? Maybe they'd found each other while hiding in the forests of Poland. I imagined they had fought heroically together and helped save other Jewish families that hid in the woods. There was a possibility I could learn some personal stories about the both of them.

Eventually I came back to reality. Lea's suggestion seemed so incredulous that my expectations dwindled.

It was useless trying to sleep. I got out of bed at the crack of dawn, wrote a list of questions for Lea and left them in my office. Then I set the kitchen table and began preparing our breakfast.

Entertaining guests in my home is something that I'd missed out on when I was younger. Before I'd invite a friend, I would have to figure out when my dad would be gone and then forewarn my mother and brothers to hold off fighting with him, if by chance he should come home. While I'd be in my bedroom with a friend, I'd always be vigilant listening to the sounds outside my walls. My nerves were fried by the time my company had left. After a while, I gave up on having friends in my home. As I raised my children, one of my priorities was to ensure that our home would always be a welcoming place for their friends.

This morning, as I was keeping busy (my remedy for reducing anxiety) I was having eerie thoughts about Arie Kaplan, this mysterious spirit. What if Lea summoned up a ghost or possibly a demon? Dabbling in the supernatural and looking for a strange soul might be dangerous. Who knew? Maybe this spirit would cast a spell on me? Ever since the home-invasion, I'd been cautious about who I allowed into my home and that included unknown spirits.

It would be another hour until Lea was scheduled to arrive. I filled the time by doing laundry and organizing cabinets...all while hoping to erase unpleasant thoughts.

At 9 the doorbell rang. Lea greeted me with her cheerful smile. We hugged like we were sisters. Lea once mentioned that in a past life, we actually were sisters and that is why we're closely connected—despite our vast cultural differences in this lifetime.

The teapot whistled. We sat down at the kitchen table. I made Lea hot herbal tea and for myself a steaming cup of coffee. We noshed on some bagels, lox, and cream cheese. I served homemade mandelbread. This wasn't the sort of breakfast that Lea normally ate, but I knew she enjoys all sorts of ethnic foods and that morning I'd had a craving for brined salmon.

Bobby popped in for a few minutes to say hello.

Lea and I usually had our sessions on my garden terrace, just off the kitchen. Bobby, being a master gardener, had created an alluring, colorful oasis with bright red flowering mandevillas that grew 10 feet high and covered the brick walls. Our planters were filled with showy tropical flowers of red and pink hibiscus. Bobby's intent was to bring some of the Jamaican landscape to our garden. The butterflies, bees, dragonflies, and hummingbirds were all welcome guests in this little paradise. Having open skies and tree top views allowed us to see the majestic sunrises and sunsets. It's a magical world there during the daytime, and when evening descends, dim white lights come on and we enjoy our private view of the moon and the constellations.

I mentioned to Lea that when I was growing up, my father never allowed us to bring flowers into our home. He was repulsed by them. How could he, or anyone for that matter, hate a flower? They simply add beauty and joy in our lives. I speculated that because my dad was frugal with money, he didn't want to spend a dollar on something that was going to die. But my mom had planted flowers in the front of our condo and a vegetable garden in the backyard. Every summer I couldn't wait until she'd pick the ripe rhubarb, boil the magenta stalks with tons of sugar, and bake the best tasting pies.

After Lea and I had finished breakfast, we carried our hot beverages to my office. She was still chilled from the cold and damp weather, so I gave her a pair of soft knit socks and a throw blanket. She sat at my desk making herself comfortable as I sat nearby on the sofa and fidgeted with a pen while reviewing my questions. Lea noticed that I was becoming more anxious and said, "Let's see what today's hour will bring. There's nothing to be nervous about. Just relax, take notes and I will record the session."

She asked me to take a few deep breaths to quiet my mind and relax my body. Then she closed her eyes to recite a prayer. She said, "Dear God, we ask that you bring the highest information for Karen's soul growth. Surround us with love, light, healing, wisdom, and truth. We are here today to call upon the spirit of a man called Arie Kaplan, whose identification was used by Karen's father during World War II and for the remainder of his life. Please help us bring forth his energy. As always we thank you for your assistance."

Lea always begins with an intentional prayer of safety and protection before each session. It actually helps ground me so that I can focus on the upcoming hour. Then she enters this meditative state and conveys a message. While she channels, she can go in and out of this trance-like phase so that I can ask her questions and she can offer explanations. Sometimes when she channels, the spirit will speak through her. At other moments, she hears the messages and relays them to me. To this day, I am mystified that she can communicate with the spirit energies in other realms. Sometimes I wish I had her abilities so that I too would have direct contact with my mother and brother.

Then, Lea spoke: "Greetings dear one, it is I, Archangel Michael, and I am here to escort the one named Arie Kaplan. He has agreed to come forward to speak. I will step back, as he has much to say. He is nervous and shy but will try his best to answer your questions most directly."

Archangel Michael had come through many channeling sessions when I'd sit with Lea. He often brought inspirational messages.

As Lea spoke, my mind wandered.

The name "Michael," in Hebrew, means, "who is like God." Angel encounters are many throughout the Torah and other Jewish texts. During my years of Jewish education, I'd read stories about angels appearing before Hagar, Abraham's maid-servant, and Sarah, Abraham's wife. The one I recall best was when the angel was informing them that they would have a child, and that their descendants would be numerous.

Jacob dreamed of angels and eventually wrestled with one.

While the Hebrews were enslaved in Egypt, the infamous Angel of Death descended onto the firstborn Egyptians and smote them all.

Every Friday night after the sabbath candles are lit at sunset, Jews all throughout the world usher in the day of rest by singing a beautiful melody welcoming the angels of God into their homes.

I never gave much thought about these beings of light until I met Lea. She told me that she works with many angels and spirits that are dedicated to help humanity achieve its potential. For me, this angelic realm is hard to grasp, but the information that Lea presented during our sessions had been quite insightful.

Then, as she felt the spirit come to her, Lea said, "My name is Arie Kaplan. I was born as the third child of my parents, Henrietta and Joseph Kaplan. We lived in a very small village and we were Polish. My parents were small business merchants in the town of Rajgròd. We were very much simple people and when the war broke out, I was called to serve in the armed forces. Since I had a small disability, I thought that it would prohibit me from going into the army. I had a weak left leg and was born with a limp. It was similar to polio, but I believe it is called a clubfoot. Because I was not very fast on my feet, my mother always tried to protect me from hardship. She was terrified when I was sent into the army. She was afraid I would get killed and never come home. Her fears manifested."

My heart skipped a beat when the spirit said that he was from Rajgròd. I could feel the tiny hairs on my arms stand up. There was hope, I thought, that I would get concrete information about him and my father. If this spirit lived in Rajgròd, then my father must have known him. In those small villages everyone seemed to know each other. Maybe they were friends after all. I couldn't wait to hear more details about him and his relationship with my dad before the war. I continued taking notes as Lea was relaying the message from him.

"I am very sorry that when I died, I had great anger within my heart. I never wanted to go into the service for I was scared and not very aggressive. Because I witnessed so many atrocities during the war, a great deal of rage ignited inside of me and I did not behave normally. When you are forced to fight, it makes you angry, it makes you aggressive and it makes you do things you might have never done."

To me, this spirit sounded like he'd suffered from post-war mental trauma, just like my father had. My attention shifted back to Rajgròd. All I could think about was that this spirit came from my father's village. I looked directly at Lea but asked the spirit, "Can you tell me more about your family life and your childhood in Rajgròd?"

"We were well-liked in our village and no one seemed to really trouble us. I had two older sisters. They were both married. Their husbands became soldiers in the war. My father came from a hard-working family and my mother brought kindness and love into our home. When the city was invaded, my parents were spared and not taken into custody because they provided food for the soldiers from their small grocery store. My sisters were forced to relocate up north, and their husbands could not protect them. I am trying to answer as best as I can, but this is all new to me, yet I have come to assist you," said Arie, the spirit.

Now my heart was racing. My mind felt as if it was going to explode with questions for him. "I appreciate you coming forward today and sharing your story," I said. "Can you tell me where your family store was located? My grandmother, Beila Szteinsaper, lived next to a grocery store in the center of town. She also owned a farm a few miles west of Rajgròd, down the main road. Did you know my father or the Szteinsaper family?"

The spirit responded, "My father opened his merchant shop in 1914. It appears that things are a bit different now in Rajgròd. It was a general store, just across the road from the railroad station. My father and mother both worked in the store seven days a week. We were not lazy people, and we didn't have a lot of time for leisure. At the end of each day my mother cooked dinner for all of us. Nearby was the lake and my family and I would often picnic there. We were happy and had a fair amount of money for everything we needed. I was shy and did not have a girl-friend yet. But I would enjoy being with my male friends. We would go swimming in the lake and sled down the hills."

"Wait a second," I said to Lea, "this is not making any sense. Lea, did you say railroad station? There is no railroad station in Rajgròd. There is the lake and a hill as he describes."

Lea responded, "Yes, I'm seeing train tracks and an old station building."

"I've been to Rajgròd twice. I'm certain there is no train station there. There's a small bus station in the center square adjacent to my grandmother's home and a store nearby."

"Would you like me to continue and see if Arie can clarify?" Lea asked.

"Sure," I said, even though I was losing faith.

"I never knew of your father or his family in Rajgròd," the spirit said. "We lived on the northern end of the village. Maybe your father lived in the southern region and did not come to our store. My parents might have known your family, but I did not. You see, I only helped my father after school. We were partly Jewish but not religious. My dad was a German Jew. He married my mother who was Greek Orthodox. My dad did not mind that my mother was not Jewish. We followed more of my mom's religious traditions though my father shared some Jewish customs with me inside our home. He was mainstream and independent and did not discriminate against anyone. I was raised that if you are a good person, then your religion, culture, and nationality should not matter. We were a proud and well-respected, working-class family but in many ways, we were considered a bit richer than others, because my father owned the store, and this is where people came to get their food and supplies."

"Are there records of your family?" I asked.

"Yes, you can find records of my family. I was born 10 miles east of Rajgròd on June 14, 1923," said the spirit.

"How do you spell your name?" I asked.

"A R J E I and K A P L A N," he said. "My family changed it or shortened it because it was hard to pronounce. I was named after my uncle and paternal great grandfather. In the town where I was born, my father was mayor for a couple of terms. He had influence in the area."

From that point on, I had decided to write his name as he'd spelled it, Arjei Kaplan. Then I asked him, "What was the name of the town where you were born?"

"Karen, it is too difficult for me to pronounce," said Lea.

I asked the spirit, "Can you tell me why your family moved to Rajgròd?"

The spirit answered, "My father wanted to live near his father. My grandfather opened up a wood carving business. He made furniture and provided many house items for our family."

"Did your sisters have children?" I asked.

"My sisters did not have children so there is no continued lineage. They and their husbands were all killed by the Nazis. My parents did not know what happened to me, and my mother suffered most deeply, as did my father. My mother and father were spared because of their store, which makes me feel good," said Arjei the spirit.

I asked, "The Catholic church is located in the northern part of Rajgròd. Was your store close-by?"

Lea said, "He doesn't remember a church."

I said, "But the church is the tallest building in sight. You can see it from the other end of the village."

The spirit said, "There was the train station, as I said before on the northern edge of town. Before the war, I would watch people go by, hour upon hour. I would wait underneath the lamp post for this special young lady that I liked and yet that never happened because I was sent off to war."

Extremely disappointed, I said, "Lea, I'm sorry but I don't believe this information is accurate. I don't know who you're speaking to, but I'd like to end this session."

"Of course," said Lea and she closed with a prayer.

I sat there feeling confused because I couldn't make sense of this reading.

Lea said, "I'm sorry that this session wasn't helpful, Karen. I don't know what to tell you, but I'm sure you'll figure this out."

"I really appreciate your efforts," I said, "but I'm not sure what direction I will take now."

Lea gathered her things and left for her next appointment. I gave her a travel mug with hot tea, some extra mandelbread, and a great big hug.

Later that day, I shared the experience with Bobby. He doesn't discredit this paranormal world of spirits, yet he doesn't believe in it either. He says he needs valid proof of their existence. He once said that I speak to my dead relatives more than he speaks to his living ones. It was kind of funny, but true.

"It looks like I'll never discover the secret of my father's past," I said.

"Take a break for now," he said, "you've been at this for several months. Something will come your way. We both know that you always manage to figure things out. Have a little more patience."

"Somehow, someway," I said, "I am determined to solve the identity of this stranger."

During that session with Lea, I had no doubt that she was talking to a spirit named Arjei Kaplan, but his story did not make sense. Maybe there was some form of mis-communication? Lea happens to be exceptionally accurate about uncovering informa-tion from the past because the events have already occurred. Unlike the future, where it has not been determined yet, it can be subject to change based on one's free will.

I decided to do some digging on the internet. For the next three weeks, I spent my waking moments searching each day for answers. I looked at detailed satellite pictures of train tracks from Warsaw and Bialystok leading to Rajgròd. None of the trains connected to my father's village. They veered several miles west or north of Rajgròd. Maybe the tracks were bombed during World War II? Then I began researching the history of the Rajgròd Catholic church and discovered that this colossal edifice was erected between 1906 and 1912, long before World War II, and before Arjei's father opened up his store in Rajgròd.

Exasperated, I was ready to give-up, but at the last minute I Googled the words "Rajgròd Train Station." What appeared next was an image of a four-car passenger train standing in front of a station made of beige bricks. There were signs posted on two sides of the building saying RAJGRÒD. A lamp post stood close by the tracks, just as Arjei had described.

Goosebumps spread up and down my arms and my heart was thumping so fast, I thought it was going to explode. I'd never seen this when I traveled to Rajgròd. I jumped out of my chair screaming, "I can't believe this! Bobby, come look! I found the Rajgròd train station. This is unreal!"

Bobby stared wide-eyed at the computer screen as he viewed the picture of the train. He, too, was shocked at my discovery. I had been to Rajgròd twice and was absolutely certain the only way to travel there was by car or bus. But this is nonsensical, I

Rajgròd Catholic Church in my father's town.
Photo credit: Janusz Karwowski.

thought. I am 99.9 percent positive that there was no train station in Rajgròd.

Doing further research on the internet, I discovered that there are two villages in Poland called Rajgròd. Arjei Kaplan, the spirit, came from a small town located in northwest-central Poland, in a remote area of the countryside in the province called Pomerania. The village is so small that it took me hours to find it on Google Maps as I tirelessly kept on enlarging the satellite pictures. I also noticed that there was no church or any large municipal building in the area.

Rajgròd train station in Poland in Arjei's town.
Photo credit: CC BY SA (GRAD), Wikimedia Commons.

Lea was able to conjure up the spirit of a deceased man called Arjei Kaplan who spoke about his family and his hometown of Rajgròd, Poland. What a strange coincidence that my father and this spirit came from a town with the same name. But what was their connection?

Then I researched the villages that were 10 miles directly east of Arjei's hometown of Rajgròd. I wanted to know where he was born and to see if I could find records to verify all this information. There were several villages in the area to consider so I wrote down a list of names and planned to ask Arjei the next time we spoke.

Now I was eager to hear more from this spirit.

CHAPTER 12

MISCHLING

ॐ

Lea left town and traveled back to Florida. I couldn't wait another month until she returned to Chicago, so we decided to do a FaceTime appointment for April 12th.

When we were face-to-face on the screen I said, "Lea, this is one of the craziest stories that have ever happened to me. I'm glad I was persistent and figured out this mystery of Rajgròd."

"I had full faith in you," she replied. "It was very clear what I had heard and seen, but it took your detective skills to solve this conundrum."

There were so many questions I had for Arjei, but I mostly wanted to learn about his connection with my dad, and I was also curious about his service in the army. Had he lived in my father's hometown, which was close to the Russian border, he might have been sent to the Russian front to fight against the Nazis. Some Jews joined the partisans in the forests, an irregular military group, which engaged in guerrilla warfare and sabotage against the Wehrmacht, the German army.

But Arjei lived closer to the German border, so he must have been a soldier in the Polish Armed Forces. I read that the Polish resistance movement in World War II, along with the Polish army, was the largest underground movement of occupied Europe. They were able to save more Jews in the Holocaust than any other government or Western ally organization. The underground provided military intelligence to the British and bombed the German supply lines.

I took out my pen and paper, ready to take notes while Lea set up her recorder. Then she began with the usual prayer of protection and guidance and spoke as a channel. Archangel Michael once again appeared and said, "Arjei Kaplan, the young soldier is here today. We are helping him hold the frequency so he can stay longer. His energy has not quite acclimated to the earthly plane."

"Thank you," I said.

"Karen," Lea said, "it appears that Arjei is still very timid. He is afraid that people will learn about his life story and judge him. He sees that you might be writing a book about him and your father. Yet he has come here to help you understand and will try to answer all your questions."

"I'm in no position to judge anyone. I just want to learn more about his life during World War II," I said. "Besides, one book is more than I thought I would ever write."

Lea went on with channeling his spirit and I heard Arjei say, "At the beginning of the war, a Polish sergeant, who knew my father when he was mayor, came to our home and forced my parents to keep the store open for the soldiers. In return, my parents were protected. I was 17 years old at that time and was expected to enlist in the army. The sergeant promised my parents that I would not serve on the front lines. Instead, I would be his personal assistant, washing his clothes and cooking for him. He reassured my parents that he would take care of me. I was led to be a foot soldier, holding a very minimal position with no rank or stripes.

"My responsibilities included hauling and carrying the artillery and weapons for my troop. The soldiers thought I was stupid because of my club foot. I stumbled and fell a lot and was punished for not being quick. They treated me like a slave and considered me a cripple and mentally handicapped.

"I went to serve because of my civic duty but never wanted to leave my parents. My father forced me. It would have been a shame on my family if I did not go," said his spirit.

"What an awful experience," I thought. "He was treated so brutally while serving his country."

"After 10 months I couldn't tolerate my service any longer. I had enough of being beaten and humiliated. It took me another nine months to escape. The soldiers thought I was naive but once I gained their trust, I fled."

"You deserted the Polish army?" I asked.

"I wasn't in the Polish army," said Arjei's spirit.

"What do you mean?" I asked. "What army did you serve?"

"I was called to serve under the German regime."

"What? You were fighting with the Nazis?" I was confused.

"Yes, I was forced to serve in the Wehrmacht."

"Oh my God! You were a Nazi!" I was caught off-guard. After I collected my bearings, I lowered my voice and asked, "How does a Pole, who is part Jewish, end up in the German army?"

"I thought I was fighting to free our people and on the side of the freedom fighters! But the Polish sergeant purposely misled us, and the German soldiers tricked us. I learned quickly that I was being called to be a part of the eventual extermination of the Jews in Auschwitz. I was taken by foot to the German Prisoners of War camp and trained to harm our own people." Through Lea's voice, I heard the spirit crying out.

Now I was incredulous. "That doesn't make any sense. This story is ludicrous. Hitler would not be drafting Jews into the army."

There was an explanation. Arjei went on: "We were forced to turn against our own Jewish brethren. We were tricked. Just like the children in the Hitler Youth Movement who turned against their own families, they were trying to indoctrinate us and turn us against our people. Jewish commanders in the Polish Army, who were trying to stop Hitler, along with high ranking Polish officers and Polish Catholic priests, were all imprisoned at Auschwitz. I was assigned to them. My job was to tie their hands behind their backs and bind their feet together to prevent them from running away. I wanted nothing to do with this. I'm not a bad person. We, too, were victims and had no control over our lives. I do not want any shame upon my family's name. Please, you need to understand."

I said to Lea, "I'm trying to comprehend this story but it's very confusing."

"Let him continue to speak," Lea said, "maybe we'll learn more." A minute passed, and then Arjei returned.

"I was assigned to fetch water for the prisoners from a stream outside the camp because there was no electricity or running water there. It was strenuous work. One day we were told that the streams were full because of the rains and I grabbed my jugs and knife and left to gather the water. It was late in the afternoon and I decided it was time to escape. I'd have a full night of running, and as I watched the sunset, I headed east. I also circumvented my trail to ward off the German Shepherd guard dogs that hunted the runaway prisoners. But I didn't think they would pursue me. After all, the soldiers did not care about me or my life. I had not planned well since I brought very little food but was able to eat some berries in the forest. I was so frightened, and ran for three days. On the third night, the freezing rain, sleet, and hail poured non-stop. The winds were howling, and the temperature dropped. I was not dressed properly. Tired, cold, and hungry, I ran and ran farther into the woods. My foot gave out. I stumbled over a rock and hit my head. Unconscious, I lay there with a cracked skull, dying, all alone," said Arjei's spirit.

Now I was filled with compassion for the spirit of Arjei. "What a horrible way to die," I said.

Lea said, "I'm sensing that Arjei is not able to continue much longer. Any last questions?"

"Yes, one more, please. I have a list of villages that might be your birthplace," I said.

"I have helped guide you to find my hometown," Arjei said. "Please say the names or spell them."

"Lea, I can't pronounce these names. Here's the spelling, B Y D O G S Z C Z," I said. "No, that's not it," said Lea.

"M R O C Z A," I spelled.

"No continue on," said Lea.

"S A M S I E C Z Y N E K," I said.

"Go on."

"O S T R O W O," I said.

"Yes, that is it! When you will search the town records you will see my family name. This is where my father was mayor. There is an old library building that contains these records. If it is not computerized then you must go there," he said.

"One more quick question. How is it that you and my father came from the only two towns in Poland with the same name?"

"It is just a coincidence," said the spirit, "the angels in heaven are laughing."

Lea said, "His energy is fading but he promises to return to help you."

"I must go now. I must go," said Arjei.

This session ended. Once again, I was left perplexed.

Now I knew I had to do some research about Polish people serving under the Nazi regime, and I scanned the internet. To my dismay, I discovered that Poles of various ethnic backgrounds were conscripted into the Wehrmacht at the beginning of World War II. They became pawns or foot soldiers having very little rank in the army. Indeed, they were called upon to do the dirty work for the German soldiers.

Yet, I was still conflicted because Arjei was partially Jewish. "Hitler would never allow a Jew in his army," I thought.

Then I learned that within the German army there were roughly 150,000 foot soldiers who were called *mischling*, meaning they were either half Jewish, or had at least one Jewish grandparent. These soldiers came from two western provinces in Poland that were annexed by Germany: Pomerania and Upper Silesia.

Arjei Kaplan lived with his family in the province of Pomerania.

How ironic that these young soldiers fought for the Third Reich, a government that deprived them of their rights and sent their families to the gas chambers. Many, like Arjei Kaplan, were conscripted and had no choice but to become cannon fodder.

Millions of Jews, Poles, and Slavs were forced to work in the Nazi slave-labor camps to help the German war industry and boost its economy by producing supplies. They repaired bomb-damaged railroads and bridges and worked on farms. Prisoners in the work camps lived in deplorable conditions with minimal food rations. Millions died.

Bobby's father was transported to a lumber camp where he spent the remaining years of the war. Just like Arjei, Bobby's dad had no choice but to aid Germany.

Even German citizens were victims of their own regime. Like Arjei had mentioned, the Hitler Youth Movement, a group of boys aged 14 to 18, were

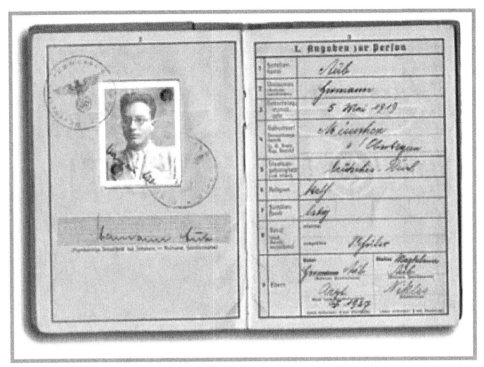

Military service identification for a *mischling*.

indoctrinated into the Nazi ideology and forced to spy on their own families. Many young boys were attacked and punished if they did not join the movement. Towards the end of the war, many of the Hitler Youth were conscripted into the army at age 17, and if or when they did not follow orders, they, too, were killed.

Arjei had said that he was forced to tie up the Polish officers, Catholic priests, and Jewish commanders in Auschwitz. When Bobby and I visited Auschwitz, we learned that this camp was first established for those particular inmates. The prisons in Poland were filled to capacity so the Nazis had built this Prisoners of War camp and transported their victims to Auschwitz to be tortured and murdered. The Poles were some of the first prisoners in Auschwitz, the first human experiments, and the first victims that were gassed to death. Later on, Auschwitz became one of the largest extermination camps for the final solution—Hitler's plan for the genocide of the European Jews. In this killing center, the Roma, homosexuals, Russian prisoners of war, and other subhuman nationalities were also murdered.

Still mystified about how my father had obtained Arjei Kaplan's identification, I was intent to get some answers the next time I communicated with him through Lea. She and I set up another session, just one week later, on FaceTime.

In the meantime, I emailed the tour guide, Maciej, in Poland to see if he could help me verify records of Arjei's family from Ostrowo. After several weeks of exploring, Maciej said that the only way to get to the records was to go there in person. It looked like it could take years before I would get any answers through email.

All throughout the week, I couldn't stop thinking about Arjei's tormented life as a soldier in the Wehrmacht and his tragic death in the woods. His shame was evident as he reluctantly divulged the details of his living nightmare. His pain felt so real and raw and he seemed to be suffering from his past.

In retrospect, I wish there was something that I could have said at that time to make him feel better and help him move beyond his anguish. In that session, I was so overwhelmed by his story that my focus was only on trying to make sense of what he had said.

CHAPTER 13

TRAPPED

श्र

Lea was just as eager as I was to learn more about Arjei's life. When we were back on the FaceTime call, Lea said, "Conscripted in Hitler's army was devastating for him."

"I can't even imagine," I said. "It would be like a Black slave being forced to fight on the side of the Confederacy during the Civil War. Insanity!"

Lea agreed. "War traumatized Arjei's life, and generations of people continue to be affected by what occurred years ago. We still have not learned the lessons of war."

Her comment made me think about the recent and senseless wars the United States had participated in since World War II. Our soldiers had always come home damaged with Post-Traumatic Stress Disorder, PTSD. Many are and were unable to function in society. Some who had survived combat returned home to commit suicide. Their families still carry this pain from decades ago.

I asked Lea, "Before we begin our session, can you explain what Arjei meant when he said that he directed me to find his village?"

"It was through telepathy. Arjei gave you a download of insight. Karen, have you ever had an epiphany? Angels and spirits inspire us by sending words, sounds, and images through our energy field. This is just one of many ways they help us on Earth."

That was very kind of him, I thought. I'll have to let him know how much I appreciate his efforts.

Lea led me back to the task by saying, "Now let's focus on this upcoming hour with Arjei. Is there anything special you would like to know today?"

"Yes, how did my father attain Arjei's identification, and did they have any connection during the war?"

"Let's find out." Lea grounded herself, completed her prayer, and began to channel. "Arjei is present," said Archangel Michael through Lea. "There is more to his story and I will continue to help him maintain this earthly frequency."

"It sure takes a village," I said, and added, "even in heaven."

Lea said, "I'm sensing some turmoil within Arjei. This is so very strange. Give me a moment."

Turmoil? What is going on with him? I started feeling shaky as if I'd just finished a double shot of espresso. I wasn't sure if I could handle any more surprises from this spirit. I sat in silence, waiting for Lea to continue. It took several minutes for him to speak through her.

"It was in May of 1943 when I died of a head trauma, hypothermia, and starvation. My leg was broken, and I was unconscious. At 19 years old, I lay on the frozen ground, in the woods, all alone. I died with bitterness and anger in my heart toward Hitler and Germany. All I wanted was to return home to my family, work in the store, and eventually marry and have children. I called out to God, but no one heard me."

Lea…Arjei…stopped talking.

After a few moments, I said, "Arjei, please go on."

"Your father found me in the morning, face down on the ground. He was in a state of fear and shock. He shook me but my body did not move. Yet, I was startled. Then he turned me over. I noticed that icicles had formed on my hair and beard overnight. He ransacked my clothes. I tried punching and fighting him off, but I couldn't defend myself. I looked down at my body, put two and two together, and realized that I was dead. Then I had enough sense to know that my spirit was out of my body and I had remained earth-bound."

"Is that when my father found your ID?"

"Yes, he found my small pouch that contained my army identity card along with my knife," he said, "then he put the pouch inside his pants pocket. He removed my jacket, shirt, and boots. We were a similar size, so my clothes fit him fine. As I said before, your father was in a state of desperation, hysteria, and fright. He was traumatized, not grounded or in his body. He was partially desensitized, and his soul was in fragments. His energy field was easily vulnerable."

Now entranced by this delivery of important information, I paid attention to every word.

"I made a quick decision," said Arjei, "just like a flea that hops on the back of a horse, I merged, and attached my energy to your father's energy field. He didn't realize what had happened. I thought your dad could take me back to Rajgròd. This may sound strange to you, but it was easy jumping into his body."

"You're a dybbuk!" I gasped. A dybbuk is a ghost or a wandering, demonic soul that possesses the body of a living person. A dybbuk can talk through the mouth of its host, and perhaps cause severe mental illness. I always thought this was Jewish folklore, a bunch of superstitious legends from centuries long ago.

"Call me what you like. Your father's emotions, along with my demeanor and anger, all intertwined. He was possessed with my energy. So, my emotional and

"Dybbuk," Ephraim Moses Lilien, 1908.

109

mental state coupled with his own traumatic experiences intensified. This is why your father became enraged," he said.

This is beyond insanity, I thought. I was speechless.

Arjei continued and said, "When we left my body on the ground in the woods, we ran and ran. Your father had a good set of lungs. I've never experienced running at great speeds. I felt settled and less scared because I was with him. I know this might be hard to believe, but it is the truth. I guess you can call me an entity or a spirit possession."

I said to Lea, "I'm really trying to digest this story."

Lea said, "In all my years of channeling, I've never dealt with an entity possession."

Then I asked Arjei, "Did anyone ever find your body?"

"No one ever found me except for the animals in the forest. I was glad I had attached to your father at that time, because witnessing the vultures feeding off my decayed body would have disgusted me."

"How long did you stay in my father's body?"

"Until he took his last breath."

I was shocked. "You were with him while he was dying in the hospital?"

Arjei said, "I wanted to leave his energy field all throughout his life, but I was trapped. Every time he did something awful, I tried to free myself from him. Remember those bursts of anger? One moment he was civil and the next moment he was explosive. It was also me, trying to escape. I was releasing my own frustrations and fury within him. I am sorry that I merged energies. Please, please forgive me. I know to never do this again. I refused to believe in God when I died. Your father rejected God, too, even though it appeared he may have espoused his religion. We could not be helped by the angels because we were two lost souls that intertwined energies. Following these uncontrollable bouts of violence, your father would be remorseful; he didn't understand what had happened. It was like having had a split personality or multiple personalities. I'm surprised he did not go crazy after all those years."

"Oh my God!" I said out loud, "this is frickin' crazy!" I didn't know what to believe. When I finally calmed down, I realized that Arjei seemed to truly understand my father's mercurial behavior. He also said he was partially responsible for it.

But did Arjei ever realize that I was always on edge, wondering when I would have to dash into my bedroom, hide in my closet, and cover my ears as my father assaulted my mother and brothers? Did he ever notice that I would run down the back stairwell of our condo into the yard waiting anxiously for the fighting to subside? Did Arjei recognize that I was always on edge when having a friend in my home, wondering if my father would explode in front of me? My dad was like a ticking time bomb just waiting to detonate.

Some of those most unnerving moments happened in public.

My mother wanted my father to attend my school functions. Each time I felt my stomach tightening and twisting. I was petrified that my father would start a fight with her in front of all my classmates and their families.

Was this spirit ever aware that my symptoms of startle reflex began during those childhood years and the effects continue to linger on today? Loud, harsh and abrupt noises along with anything or anyone that moves quickly into my space startles me. It could simply be a butterfly, a cat, or someone's voice that will scare me, and I'll grab the person who is at my side or scream when I'm alone. My poor husband often had to take the brunt of these overreactions as my symptoms worsened after the home invasion.

Lea said, "He apologizes for transposing his life unto your father's life. He never meant to harm or hurt anyone. His spirit is in a resting place, still trying to receive aid. He has volunteered to help you understand what happened and wants your forgiveness."

"Forgiveness? A spirit is asking me for forgiveness? This whole story is bizarre!"

"Do you forgive him?"

"Lea, can we take a break here? I need a few minutes to think about what I've just heard."

I sat for a while with my thoughts. Could Arjei's story be true? Are entity attachments real? I'd heard of exorcisms performed in the Catholic church for people who thought they were victims of demonic possession, but I never believed in it or gave it much thought.

The first time I had ever heard of evil attachments was when I was 11 years old—when the iconic horror movie "The Exorcist" was playing in movie theaters. It was based on a true story of a 12-year-old-girl who was possessed by a mysterious evil entity. Her mother asked two priests for help. At that time, many moviegoers were shocked and horrified by the film and couldn't sleep for days. This is all I really knew about it; I had never seen it because I was (and still am) squeamish.

What if Arjei was speaking the truth? And what if he had never invaded my father's body? My life could have turned out differently. I might have had an emotionally healthier father that doted on me and loved me. I might have made better choices as an adult. But I just couldn't dwell on the "what ifs" anymore. I'd moved well beyond that way of thinking and had taken full responsibility for my own choices.

Yet, this young soldier's spirit didn't resemble an evil entity. He seemed honest and sincere when he spoke through Lea. He was apologetic for his past actions and sought forgiveness from me. Arjei meant no harm toward my father, my family, or me. He was a victim of the war, just like my dad. I wasn't going to hold onto any grudges; the war had happened over 80 years ago. Yet, Arjei seemed troubled by his past choices and had difficulty moving forward.

I told Lea that I was ready to continue the session and said to Arjei, "Of course, I forgive you…but you don't need my forgiveness. You did what you thought was best under those dire circumstances. I hope you can learn to forgive yourself, so you can move beyond the past. Holding onto the pain doesn't benefit you, it only hurts you. I've learned that letting go and forgiving has helped me heal. You deserve to be happy, Arjei. Please do this for yourself."

Arjei said, "I regret that I didn't know how to move myself into the light or heaven. It was not your dad's fault that he had all these personalities, mental illness, and trauma. He had so many problems. I see the error in my ways, but I cannot change the course of time."

Lea said that Arjei was having trouble holding his energy and he could not stay too much longer. She asked, "Any last questions?"

"Why did my dad assume your name?"

Lea said, "He thought it was safer to switch names. Your father knew the men that murdered his family and was terrified that they would hunt him down and kill him. So, he buried the name Avrum Szteinsaper and created a new identity to deter them from ever finding him. Being a foot soldier also gave your dad more neutrality and sympathy if he were to get caught. Your dad saw the importance of my army identification and it helped him survive the war."

At that, Arjei was no longer present.

Lea said, "Karen, he wasn't able to hold the frequency any longer. I'm surprised he was able to stay as long as he did. Would you like to continue your sessions with Arjei, or are you satisfied with the information?"

I thought, "If Arjei indeed possessed my father's body, then he can explain how my father survived in the forests. He might help me understand aspects of my dad's personality" Then, looking at Lea, I said, "Yes. I have more questions for him. Can you explain what Arjei meant when he said my father's soul was in fragments?"

"Part of your father's soul, or pieces of his energy field, had left his body because the pain of witnessing his family being murdered was too overwhelming for him to bear. His soul splintered for his survival. You can compare this to someone who has unconsciously repressed memories from a traumatic episode during their childhood. The blockage is to protect them from the high stress level of the incident and to protect them from the extreme emotions of fear, anger, and depression. The brain is telling the body that it's too difficult to handle."

Lea's explanation led me to think about the home invasion I experienced. I told Lea that when I awoke to the two hoodlums standing in my bedroom and pointing their pistols at me, it felt like an out-of-body experience.

"That is a common phenomenon when one experiences a shocking ordeal," she said. "That is why Holocaust survivors, along with rape victims and abused children, often are unable to come forward until many years later when they are ready to deal with their past."

"When I was a little girl, I remember learning a prayer in school called *Modeh Ani* which means 'I thank you.' Upon awakening, before stepping out of bed, I would recite this two-sentence prayer in Hebrew to express gratitude to God for restoring my soul each morning. My rabbis taught me that while sleeping, God takes 1/60th of our soul and returns it to us when we awake. Does part of the soul leave the body while we sleep?"

"Yes, it can. One time I experienced sleep paralysis. I woke up but was unable to move or speak for a couple of minutes. It was frightening. At that time, I didn't know what had happened to me. Physicians believe that there are many causes to this occurrence, but I eventually attributed it to my soul not returning to my body. When a person sleeps, often their soul leaves their body and travels in the astral plane. Again, it's the feeling of an out-of-body experience."

This session left me wanting to know more about Arjei and my dad. I hoped his spirit was willing and able to return and spend more time with me. He had been through a cruel ordeal during the war. It seemed to have left him paralyzed with anxiety and fear. It had been over 80 years since his death in Earth time, and he was still recovering in spirit from that trauma. I wondered if there were hugs in heaven because Arjei certainly could use some. Had he been alive and sitting right next to me, I would have wrapped my arms around him to console him.

Lea was going to be traveling to Ireland to work on research for a book so we scheduled the next meeting six weeks later, when she would return to Chicago.

In the meantime, I wanted to learn about Judaism's perspective of entity invasions. One of the very first recorded cases of demonic possession might have been during the life of King Saul. After an evil spirit took over the king's body, the prophet Samuel brought young David (who was in line to be king) to King Saul so that the youth could play the lyre. David played the instrument in such a way that it drove away the demon from King Saul. David, with his lyre, could have been the very first exorcist in Jewish history.

Jews continued to perform exorcisms throughout the ages, but the practice reached its peak during the 16th century in Safed, Israel. The exorcist was usually a rabbi or someone very pious and the procedure took place inside the synagogue. A quorum of 10 men would surround the possessed person as the exorcist interviewed the demon to discover its name, personal history, and motivation for invading the other person's body—all with the hope to exorcise the demon using verbal coercion. Psalms were recited and the *shofar*, a ram's horn, was blown so its sound could help shake the devil out of the body. Though the practice of exorcism has diminished, there are a few rabbis today who still perform them.

CHAPTER 14

A FLY ON THE WALL

ও

Lea was in town for the Memorial Day weekend and came to visit me on that Monday for lunch. It was a warm spring day, perfect for the beginning of grilling season. Bobby had finished planting on the terrace, but it would take another month before the garden would be bursting at the seams with flowers and lush vines. He'd fired up the Weber grill and loaded it with salmon steaks, beef burgers, and sliced vegetables. I set the outdoor table and adjusted two patio umbrellas to create a perfect shade for the three of us. We filled our glasses with mint iced tea, enjoyed the food, and chatted for a while. Lea shared stories about her travels in Ireland and then handed me a tiny box, wrapped in gold. She said, "Go ahead and open this present. It's a memento of the magic in your life."

I unwrapped the gift and found a ceramic figure of a whimsical, red-bearded man wearing a green coat and a matching hat. I thanked her for the leprechaun and asked, "Is this little guy going to help me find the pot of gold?"

Lea said, "Karen, you have found your treasure—it's Arjei the spirit. He's learning to lower his vibration when he comes to communicate with you. Clearly, he's putting out the effort to help you." Then she added, "And you are helping him. He's feeling grateful that you have forgiven him. Your symbiotic relationship is quite magical."

By now, I felt I did have an extraordinary bond with Arjei. He was a genuine and kind soul who had been vulnerable and forthright with me. He was working hard to help me understand my father and my own past.

We cleared the table. Bobby left, and Lea and I started the next session outside. Lea sat in Bobby's comfy meditation chair, turned on her recorder to tape the session, and I grabbed a pen and paper. After she completed her prayer, she welcomed Archangel Michael. He greeted us and said that he had again accompanied my newfound friend, Arjei the spirit.

Lea said, "Arjei seems more at ease. His energy feels stronger today."

I said, "I'm happy that he's doing better. He suffered tremendously during the war and I hope he finds solace in his resting place."

Lea said that his resting place would be analogous to that of a hospital. Arjei along with many other souls who have suffered on Earth were receiving treatment by specialized staff. They were in that place to get help and heal.

I was glad to hear that there is some form of healthcare beyond death. I smiled knowing that in heaven—or on the 'other side'—everyone is cared for, not just people who have insurance. I'd also guessed that my parents also were in this type of treatment center. What I find most interesting is that my actions in this world have clearly impacted Arjei's behavior in his world. I asked Lea if she could explain how this happened.

"We are all connected. We are all one. Our energy flows through us and through everything. Your behavior affects someone else's behavior. Do you remember when I first channeled Arjei? You were quite anxious, and he was picking up your energy. He became nervous, too. He didn't know what to expect from you."

Then she told me that Arjei was waiting. He was ready to answer my questions.

I asked Arjei, "What was it like living in the forests all those years during the war? How did my father manage to survive?"

Arjei said, "Your dad ate whatever he could find. In the springtime, he picked berries and dug up underlying vegetation. But life was harsh during the winter months. When food was scarce, he used my small knife to peel bark off the trees and eat the inner lining of the trunk. He hunted and ate small rodents. Once he killed a large groundhog with my knife and drained the blood before eating the flesh of the carcass. He appeared to really enjoy it, but it was sickening.

"Your dad also seemed to have the wherewithal to be safe. In and out of the forest, he'd go into the villages like a mountain man, finding supplies and returning to the woods. He would hide behind small remote homes in the countryside and take water from the pails and fill up his pockets with food scraps. Sometimes he would approach people and forcibly get food from them, but he would always be on the move. From place to place, he would steal whatever he could find whether it be clothing, boots, or food.

I said, "In our home, my father would eat every morsel of food on his plate and drink every last drop of his beverage. It seemed that he never was able to overcome those years of starvation." Then I remembered how he would often dig through the kitchen garbage can double checking that none of us had thrown away anything valuable or edible.

Lea said, "Your father's experiences impacted him in so many ways."

Arjei continued. "Toward the end of the war, he met an elderly German couple that took care of him for a few months when he was extremely gaunt and quite ill. He slept on a cot near the fireplace. I wasn't sure if he was going to live. They didn't want him to leave but when he recovered, your dad moved on. The couple sent him to another small German town where there was a sheriff that helped many of the refugees. Similar to the Underground Railroad system for the Black slaves, there was a resistance movement for the Jews. Eventually your dad made his way to the Displaced Persons camp," he said.

"Lea, I'd like to know if Arjei was part of my family and how much influence he had on my dad?"

Arjei said, "No, I was not a part of your family. Just an outsider. Your mom was a very nice woman and a great cook. I could feel the digestion of food and savored her chicken soup, potato pancakes, and stuffed cabbage rolls. It reminded me of my mother's cooking. When your dad would smoke cigarettes and cigars and drink beers on occasion, I could feel the sensations and enjoyed that as well."

"I'm glad you appreciated my mother's cooking," I said.

Arjei said, "Karen, when you were younger, I enjoyed listening to you play the piano and sing for hours. Those were the few comfortable moments in your home. You were good natured. You had a pretty smile and reminded me of my sisters whom I missed terribly."

This information about me playing the piano was something Lea could not have known, and an example of how Arjei's awareness of my life was true.

How nice of him to compliment me. When I was a little girl, my mom saved some money and used it to buy a used piano for me. She acquired the money by shopping at the supermarket and buying additional food items. The next day she would return them so that she would have extra cash for my brothers and me. My mom would also sneak into my father's closet on Saturday mornings when he was at synagogue services and take a few dollars from his wallet—just enough so that my dad wouldn't notice that any cash was missing. At first, I thought my mother was stealing from my father, but when I was older, I realized that the money in his wallet was her hard-earned money, too.

My mom told my dad that the music teacher at the high school where she worked had given her a piano along with free piano lessons. I grew up learning to lie to my father to avoid his wrath. But that is how we were all able to survive in our household. Mom wanted me to have the things she was denied during her childhood since she was raised during the Great Depression. Owning and playing an instrument was too costly for her family back then.

That piano was an escape from the chaos in my home. At first my teacher taught me the classical pieces which my mom really enjoyed. She'd be my audience and I'd see her beaming with joy as she listened to me perform. I'd spent hours playing by ear and singing Hebrew folk songs that I learned in school. My playing would often drown out the yelling between my father and mother. In my teens, I saved money to buy sheet music from my favorite artists and bands such as Elton John, Barry Manilow, Barbara Streisand, and Chicago.

When I married, I took my piano with me and eventually played Hebrew songs for my children during the Jewish holidays. But, after the home invasion, I gave that piano away to a needy college student who was majoring in music. There was no room for it in my new condominium. I'm still grateful for that old piano which had brought me many years of enjoyment.

Arjei said, "I particularly loved being with your mom. She was a good woman and I enjoyed her company. But I missed my family so much and hated feeling like

Karen at the far right wearing a red dress.

a ghost trapped in a house. I didn't really like your family; no offense, it was just too disturbing. I called out for my parents, but I couldn't be helped. My home in Poland was filled with so much love and joy. It was hard to witness the things that went on in your home."

"Arjei was like a fly on the wall," I said to Lea.

"That's exactly right," she said.

But there were moments of happiness in our home. On Friday nights, we were all expected to eat together as we ushered in the sabbath. My mom would prepare a special meal often including homemade chicken soup and matzo balls, brisket, or a baked chicken dish, with a vegetable kugel. If she wasn't too tired from working all week, she'd surprise us with either chopped liver or sweet and sour meatballs for an appetizer.

I'd set the dining room table with our holiday dinnerware along with candle-sticks and candles, a large wine goblet filled with Mogen David wine and two whole braided challah loaves on a tray and covered with a special cloth. As soon as my dad came home, we'd all sit at the table, say the blessings and enjoy my mother's homemade meal. Following dinner, assuming there was no chaos, my brothers and I would sing *Birkat Hamazon*, the grace after meals songs, in Hebrew. When I was 5 or 6 years old, I remember sitting on my dad's lap. He was smiling and patting his hands on the table. He seemed to enjoy listening to these Hebrew melodies. Maybe those dinners reminded him of his family back home in Rajgròd. These rare moments were the few times I loved having him as my dad.

Now I asked Arjei, "Sifting through my father's files from the war, I've noticed travel documents for Australia and the United States along with an Auschwitz identification card, medical forms, processing cards, and employment papers. There are so many documents and I can't make sense of it all. Can you shed some light on this?"

Arjei said, "Your father was never in Auschwitz and he never went to Australia. After the Germans marched through the towns and forced the civilians out of their homes, he accessed the houses and took whatever he could find. Your father gathered IDs and documents so that he could falsify his name and pretend he was someone else. In those days, documents could be easily forged. If you had the papers, it was assumed to be true. Today everything is computerized, and it is more difficult to deceive others.

"When the war ended, he continued to steal. When people left papers in the restaurants, he stole them. Late at night he would go into the German pubs and hide in the corner waiting until people were drunk. Then he robbed them. He used his victims' IDs and went to their workplace and stole whatever he could find. He pretended to be them and lived off their money until he was able to transfer to the Displaced Persons camp. I remember your father connected with one merchant and took $2,000.00 from him. We lived well but we continued to hide. Your father was a kleptomaniac."

My face must have shown sadness.

Lea asked, "Are you doing ok?"

I told her I was fine. Truthfully, it was hard to hear that my dad was a chronic thief. Yet Arjei's assessment of my father seemed accurate. I recalled an incident six years prior and had to tell it. "Lea, when my dad's health was deteriorating rapidly, Barry and I had placed him in a nursing home. We put his condo up for sale and spent weeks cleaning and clearing his place. Barry and I were in my dad's bedroom when Barry found the keys to unlock the desk drawer. Inside the drawers, my brother found his bar mitzvah watch, school ring, cufflinks, along with a few other pieces of his jewelry, and some of his gold coins. Barry thought that he had lost all his jewelry when he'd moved away."

"How did your brother react?" asked Lea.

"He was fuming," I said, "I had never seen Barry so angry."

"He had every right to be upset. Your father stole from him," said Lea.

"Yes…it was awful."

Lea then asked, "Would you like to continue? Are you sure you're fine?"

"Yes, let's continue," I said, "my father lived a life of secrecy. He would leave my mother, brothers, and me all the time and we never knew where he went. I remember one night when I was little, my mom called the police because my father never came home. She also called some of our relatives to search for him. In the morning our cousin found him walking into the synagogue where he worked part-time. Back then I didn't understand the significance of him staying out all night. When my mother asked him where he went and mentioned that she called the police, he went ballistic and became physically abusive."

Arjei said, "Your father had numerous affairs. Each time he was with a woman, I turned my head away. I tried to pull out of his body, but it was futile. In your home, I tried to comfort your mom. Your dad was remorseful at times as I would try to get him to feel that way. But anyone that did not do as he wished, was punished."

I said to Lea, "Earlier I mentioned that my brother and I were cleaning out my father's bedroom. Well, I had found a large manila envelope on the top shelf of his closet. It was tucked away under multiple folders and stuffed to capacity. When I opened it, I discovered lists of women, their addresses, and phone numbers. There were also love letters and old photos of my father with many women. One photo was as recent as 1996, the year before my mother died."

Lea said, "That must have been painful to find."

"Yes, it was. In that 1996 picture, my dad and his girlfriend Bella were standing in front of a piano inside a restaurant lounge."

I met Bella soon after my mom had died. At first, my dad stayed with her a couple days a week, but later on he moved into her apartment full-time. Bella told me that they had met at the ARK, an agency that aids poor Jewish families in Chicago. My dad would often go there to pick up a free meal for himself and noticed Bella, who was taking a conversational English class at that time.

Bella was Russian. She'd come to America a few years earlier with her husband, but he had since died. My father was insistent that they have a relationship. He told her that he was a widower and was very lonely and they began to date.

Bella's English vocabulary was minimal; she spoke to my father in Russian while he answered her in Yiddish. She truly enjoyed cooking and taking care of him. When my dad went into the nursing home, I drove Bella each week to visit him. During one of those long car rides, Bella asked me when my mother had died. When I told her the truth, she was in shock. She spent the rest of the car-ride home in silence. She never brought up the subject again.

Lea said, "Your dad was deceiving her, too."

"Yes," I said and added, "Lea, when I found those love letters, I sat on my dad's bed trying to read them. My hands were trembling. I was in shock. There was one mistress in particular who knew my mother and had written obnoxious comments about her. This woman had moved from Chicago to Scottsdale, Arizona and wanted my dad to visit her.

"Apparently, during one of our very few family vacations, Howard, who had just learned to drive, along with my mother and father, all took turns driving our family out west to Arizona. Each day we dropped my dad off at the local library while my mom took us to tourist sites. None of us thought this was unusual because my dad spent hours at our neighborhood library reading the daily newspapers. We were also quite happy spending time without him. Evidently, this woman picked up my dad each day and dropped him off when the library closed."

Lea said, "He certainly lived a stealthy life."

"Why would my dad keep all these pictures and letters? Didn't he think that his children might find them one day?"

"Maybe your dad forgot about the envelope. Or maybe he couldn't throw any of it away. It was valuable to him, just like a keepsake or a trophy. It might have been a reminder of his conquest of women or maybe it helped him feel loved that all these women had desired him."

Arjei came through Lea's channel again and said, "Eventually your mother figured out that he was having affairs but there was nothing she could do."

I was thinking, "Yes. My mother was trapped. She stayed with him because she felt she had no choice. She needed the security of a home for her children and had to endure his behavior." Thankfully, today there are Jewish agencies like SHALVA in Chicago that help battered women and children. Back then many women suffered in silence.

Arjei said, "Your father had ritualistic tendencies and was obsessive compulsive. That was not me. Though our anger intermingled, I did not cause him to womanize or beat your mother and brothers. Your mother was treated like a possession. I was sickened when you were all abused.

"Your older brother Howard was more solid and resilient and handled the abuse better than your mother and brother Barry. Howard was a brilliant man with a good heart. He was the prodigal son. Your father could not get close to anyone, except Howard. He was saddened when Howard died. It was yet another loss for him. He could bear no more tragedies."

"Yes, it appeared that my dad loved Howard more than anyone in our family. He didn't shed a single tear when my mom died," I said.

Arjei said, "Barry was more sensitive and knew that your father did not like him. Karen, according to your father, you were just a girl and didn't matter."

"My father would hardly ever call me by my name. If he needed something from me, he used the word *madyl*, meaning 'girl.' I never felt acknowledged by him, yet I was grateful that he didn't curse me with appalling names that he saved for my mother and brothers. My mother and Barry received an inordinate amount of abuse in our home and in public. I always wondered why I was the only one in my family that was never physically harmed."

"Your grandmother Beila taught him to respect his sisters. He looked up to them and since you resembled his beloved sister, Yoshpe, he never laid a hand on you."

"Did my dad ever love my mother?" I asked.

"As I said before, your mother was his property. He witnessed so many atrocities during the war and carried the bitterness and anger within him his entire life. He could not control his temper. In the beginning, he fell in love with your mom. He was enamored with her beauty and gentleness. Howard was born after two years into their marriage, and your mom became needy and was easily intimidated by him. The newness wore off and that is when the abuse started. He did not believe in divorce but felt justified in having affairs to make him happy.

"It was so hard witnessing his destructive behavior toward your mother. My parents worked side-by-side. My grandfather treated my mother like a queen. Your father had no regard for women."

I affirmed this truth by saying, "He would refer to my mother, and frankly all women, as *kurvehs*, a Yiddish term for whores. My father was downright mean, controlling, and manipulative. Was he born this way or was it a result of the war? Did he exhibit any of this behavior during the war?"

"When I met your dad or vice versa, I remembered I was nervous and scared and together we struggled to survive. Your dad had psychotic breaks, screaming fits, and nightmares. He dreamed of monsters and villains. Night after night, I tried to calm him down and I was never able to sleep. It was horrifying for me to witness and experience what he saw. He suffered terribly and I tolerated his moods and upsets.

"Those early years of running made him strong. His craziness was tempered with moments of lucidity. But he was a prisoner of fear and lived in a state of depression. Once he attained my ID and I merged with him, his demeanor changed. He began to take on my dialect and the energy of my family lineage of being very proud. Your father became brazen, bold, and he took on my family's pride. With my anger and his fury, he was out of control. He made contacts with Polish families in the small villages and lied about who he was and why he was there. They promised to keep him safe. They protected us while your father stole from them. "From place to place, like a fugitive on the run, he continued this pattern. He became quite aggressive if the villagers would not obey him. I was not raised that way," Arjei said.

I felt a need to defend him. "But it was war," I said. "He was rightfully paranoid and exhibited PTSD. He never knew who might turn him in to the Nazis."

Arjei said, "Your father was not able to forgive or forget. He stabbed at least four of those villagers with my knife to get money, clothes, and food. I turned my head each time he killed. Being clever and shrewd, he knew how to manipulate them."

With conviction I said, "Every day he lived with the threat of death. He was frightened and disturbed but due to his strength and wit he survived. I will never judge my father. He did what he thought was best to remain alive."

"You are not understanding what I am saying," said Arjei. "I'm sorry but this is not what a daughter wants to hear about her father."

"What are you trying to tell me?"

"Your father was a sociopath. He relished those days of killing people. He was cruel and unethical both to people and animals. When he inflicted pain and suffering on others, there were no feelings of guilt or shame, but I sensed his excitement and pleasure. When he stole, I could feel his greed and satisfaction."

I felt a lump in my throat. I was silent and my body went numb. All I could feel was my heart pounding. In my first book, a memoir, I had written personal and detailed stories about my father and the chaos he inflicted in my home. In hindsight it was obvious that my father exhibited the characteristics of a sociopath. Arjei had hit the nail on the head.

"He was tenacious, brazen and eventually became reckless, doing whatever he wanted."

I sat, speechless, as a stream of unpleasant memories from my childhood flooded my mind. Why hadn't I figured this out before now?

Arjei said, "I tried to prevent him from attacking others by boxing with him. Your dad became delusional when he heard strange noises in his head. He had moments of tenderness and sadness, but he covered up his pain by hardening his heart. He was not born this way. But when one witnesses heinous crimes, especially toward their loved ones, it changes them. Watching his mother and sisters be bludgeoned to death turned his heart to stone. So, each time he killed, he did so with justification."

Lea stopped channeling and said, "His soul was tormented all those years. He was damaged beyond repair and couldn't move beyond the horrors of his past."

"I should have known he was a sociopath," I said.

"Don't be hard on yourself," said Lea, "you grew up in the midst of your family tumult—like being in the picture and not seeing the frame. If this is too overwhelming, we can stop now. Do you have any more questions for Arjei?"

I wanted to end the session, so I thanked her and Arjei and said I needed some time to mull over what I had just heard. I was distressed. Lea ended with a prayer and said that Arjei was willing to share more information about my father when I was ready.

After the session ended, I asked Lea to join me on a stroll towards the lake. We walked in silence down Ravine Drive, a winding side street lined with magnificent homes and enchanting canyons, filled with canopy trees, streams, and wildlife. The end of the road led to the bottom of the ravine, near a tiny neighborhood beach on Lake Michigan. We sat on two large white boulders, listening to ripples of the waves against the sandy shore. The water was as blue as the cloudless sky and made the horizon difficult to detect. I took in several deep breaths as I tried to relax.

Lea waited a few minutes then asked, "How are you feeling?

"Learning that my father was a kleptomaniac and a sociopath is pretty tough to grasp."

"I'm so sorry. Yet, Arjei was bold enough to share the truth with you."

"I really appreciated his candidness. You know that I'd prefer to hear the disturbing facts than live in oblivion. I've spent too many years not facing the truth and holding back my feelings. Living in denial is not living."

"Not everyone is willing to hear the truth. This message was given to you from someone who cares about you."

"Thank you, Lea."

"I'm referring to Arjei," Lea said.

I looked up at the vastness of the sky, smiled, and said, "Guess I have a friend in high places."

We both smiled. I was starting to feel better and we headed back home.

The next day I called Barry and shared what I had discovered with Lea. Barry was open to this spiritual world Lea had accessed, and as he listened to my story, he, too, was stunned into silence. We now understood why my father behaved so carelessly and maliciously towards our family.

It was like getting a long-awaited diagnosis after years of searching for some answers.

CHAPTER 15

RELIEVED

ॐ

As difficult as it was growing up with my father, I couldn't imagine being trapped inside his mind and body. Arjei struggled 70 more years after his death as a prisoner inside my dad.

Shaped by his shattering experiences during the war, my father shut down emotionally. His severe PTSD, anxiety, and paranoia turned him into a man with a minuscule conscience. Arjei had said that my father also took on his family's energy of fearlessness and pridefulness. This too, molded my father's personality into a focused, impulsive, abusive, and ruthless man. What a mess of unresolved emotional baggage my father had carried.

How many sociopaths live among us? I was curious because many people have endured major trauma in their lives. Not just soldiers and victims of war, but children and adults who have been raped, abused, and abandoned.

I called my friend Ross, an expert in this field, who said that according to research, people with antisocial personality disorders and psychopaths may make up one to four percent of the population. He then said, "These estimates may not be super accurate because these folks do not openly self-report their problems or answer honestly when interviewed."

"Ross, did my father understand that he was mentally unhealthy?"

"Sociopaths know who they are, but they don't see it as a bad thing. This is what makes them different from other personality disordered individuals. They know they are different, and exploit others because of it." He then added, "They are everywhere. They can be your co-workers, clergy, politicians, police officers, doctors, spouses, and children. Yet many of us do not recognize them."

"Would therapy have helped my dad?" I asked.

"Like others with antisocial personality disorders, your father never thought he had a problem and blamed everyone else for his misfortunes. Such makes a self-referral for psychotherapy unlikely. Sociopaths hardly ever experience any type of moral discomfort within themselves, which usually is a compelling factor in seeking mental health services. And if a sociopath should go to therapy, there are no known therapy techniques that are reliable and helpful in solving the disorder."

My dad and many in his generation thought therapy was for crazy people and was not even a science. Seeing a psychotherapist back then was a waste of time, energy, and money. He would have never sought help, did not want anyone to tell him differently, and continued to believe that he was a victim of this unjust world.

Ross invited me to be a guest speaker at his upcoming conference on Pathological Narcissists: Who Are They and What To Do About Them. He said that sharing my personal story of my father, a cross between a malignant narcissist and someone with antisocial personality disorder—and discussing the damaging and traumatizing influence he had on my life, would provide his attendees, of which many are licensed therapists, with a heightened awareness of this disorder. I told him that I would be willing and honored to speak. Here is the YouTube link to the presentation I gave: **https://www.youtube.com/watch?v=fPNJrx6h7yU**

By the time I again felt ready to communicate with Arjei, Lea had returned to Florida. As we started the next FaceTime session, Lea said, "You're handling these sessions very well."

"All I can do is pray that my father's soul is at peace."

I thanked Lea and told her that I was grateful for our friendship and her ability to channel Arjei. As difficult as it was to learn about these blindsiding details, I was fortunate to get a glimpse into my father's life during one of mankind's darkest and catastrophic periods in history.

"I'm happy to help you," Lea replied. "This is a unique story."

I asked, "Who is susceptible to entity attachments?"

"Children or adults who have gone through major trauma, who exhibit mental illness, and severe depression. Also, those who have extensive drug or alcohol addictions are vulnerable to attachments. Their auric fields are weakened and can be easily penetrated."

"If my father didn't know that he was possessed, how might someone know if they are harboring an entity?"

"Most people never know but there are signs—like hearing voices in one's head or having abrupt mood swings. Other signs might include having unknown sources of ailments and bruises."

I had many more questions on this subject for Lea, but I didn't want to keep my friend Arjei waiting any longer.

Lea welcomed Archangel Michael and Arjei to our FaceTime call then said, "I didn't realize that Arjei had been consulting his parents all along and they approved of him returning and revealing his story."

"Really? I didn't know that they discuss these things on the other side. I'm glad he's back with his mother and father. I miss my mom terribly, and Howard, too. Honestly, I don't miss my father," I admitted.

"When a soul crosses over, in many instances, the soul family will reunite. Your father is also getting help."

The humor I was going for with my next comment: "He's probably enrolled in anger management classes," fell flat.

"Something like that. Well, what questions do you have for Arjei today?"

"I'd like to know more about my father's life in the Displaced Persons camp."

Arjei said, "Eventually we made our way to a small DP camp in Eastern Germany. Our stay was short and then we were transferred to Bergen-Belsen, I think that is what it's called," said the spirit.

"What was it like in the Bergen-Belsen DP camp?"

"Your father was a shyster, trying to do as little work as possible. He was a manager of the refugees in the soup kitchen. People would talk there, and he would snitch on them. He couldn't trust anyone. Then he finagled his way to become the foreman reporting to the top authorities in the camp. He was a bully and bullied people out of information. He wanted a position of power and control and was never going to take orders from anyone. Does that sound like your father?"

"Yes, that clearly describes my father's nature."

Arjei said, "He taught Hebrew for a short time in the DP camp. He learned English and felt he would be safer in the United States, with more opportunities there. He was one of the first DPs to be released and put on the ship to America. He was eager to leave Europe as he was ridden with fear."

In my father's files from the war, I noticed that he had a registration and identity card that was issued on March 3, 1948. He used the name Arie Kaplan and his place of birth was Rajgròd. It had two official stamps: one with the words, "HOHNE D.P. CAMPS," and the other read "DISPLACED PERSONS ASSEMBLY." Then three months later, it was stamped again on June 8, 1948.

I had discovered that when the British liberated Bergen-Belsen concentration camp, they transferred the remaining survivors to a new Displaced Persons center and called it Hohne Camp, located about 18 miles away. The British burned Bergen-Belsen to the ground to stop the spread of typhus. Many of the extremely ill survivors were sent to the former Nazi hospital in Hohne Camp while others stayed in the Nazi barracks. It was the largest DP camp in the British zone of occupied Germany and became mostly Jewish, with a population reaching 12,000 survivors. Housing was deplorable and there was a lack of food and clothing. Yet the Jews immediately created a thriving political, cultural, and religious atmosphere by setting up schools, organizations, and places of worship. Still, the Jewish community deeply resented the name Hohne and requested that the British Authorities keep the name Bergen-Belsen in order to preserve the memory of the 70,000 inmates that perished nearby.

I understood why Arjei was unsure of the name of the camp. By the middle of 1950, most of the Displaced Persons had left and, by 1951, the camp was empty. Most of Bergen-Belsen's refugees immigrated to Israel, the United States, and Canada.

Above: Certificate of employment at the Displaced Persons camp.

Right: Registration card from Hohne Displaced Persons camp.

I said, "I'd like to trace my father's journey to Chicago. What was it like on the ship to the United States?"

Arjei said, "We were in the bow of the ship and had very little to eat which was a good thing. Your father was very sick. As the waves kept crashing onto the ship, your father kept throwing up. It felt like we were riding a bull. When we finally came onto land in New York, he collapsed."

"Why did he move to Chicago?"

"There was a lottery available that provided working opportunities in some of the major cities. So, your father left with a group of European Jews and moved to Chicago."

"Can you explain why my father married my mother, especially if he felt that way about women?"

"In order to be accepted in the United States, he had to be married. Your dad needed a pretense of a normal Jewish family life. But he could never commit to your mom."

"Arjei...while we are on the subject of marriage, I remember when I was 22 and told my father that I was engaged. He just nodded his head up and down a couple of times and left the room. He couldn't even say *mazel tov*, a Yiddish phrase for 'congratulations.' What was he thinking back then? Was he happy for me?"

"Your father was happy. Happy for himself. Happy that you were not going to be his responsibility anymore. It was one less mouth to feed at home."

"Wow," I said, "he couldn't wait to get rid of me." I knew that was the mentality of the Eastern European Jew back then. If the children could not pull their own weight in the family, they were sent away to live and find work elsewhere. Families in the rural communities could not afford to feed all their children. My father had plenty of money to feed me, but he was also extremely cheap. Wherever he could save a dime, he would. I'm still grateful that he had paid for my college tuition, but he must have felt it was time for me to support myself. At the time I became engaged, I had recently graduated college and had a job as a nutritionist at a medical company. The job also came with health insurance and a company car.

"I was happy for you." said Arjei. "Your father didn't like or dislike your husband. But your mom was crying because you were leaving her. You were her only ally and protector at home. Your brothers had already moved out. She never wanted to be alone with your dad; she was so frightened."

Tears filled my eyes. I felt so sad for my mom. She suffered until the end of her life living with my father. I should have tried harder to get her to leave my dad. I should have known the anguish and pain she felt every day. I should not have given up on her.

Arjei went on: "Your mother and I were both trapped. She would pace back and forth at home; she was so scared of him. Over the years she continued to cook, eat, and gain weight. He bullied her and called her ugly and cursed her daily in Yiddish. He was disgusted with her. But he hated himself and projected his feelings onto her."

I recalled my father calling my mom *meeskite*, meaning 'ugly thing' in Yiddish. He never called her by her name, Harriet, at home. As I grew up hearing all these obscenities, after a while, I became immune to them. I didn't realize how he chipped away at her self-esteem until I was an adult.

Lea said, "I'm hearing that when your mom passed over, she immediately went into treatment. She is well-cared for on the other side. But when she realized your father was dying, she was frightened that he might come after her. Please know that it doesn't work that way on the other side. She is doing really well now."

All I heard was that my mom was still scared of him when she was in heaven. Teardrops were running down my cheeks and I couldn't focus anymore on this session. "Lea," I said through tears, "this is by far the most difficult hour for me. It was awful living in my home and my mom suffered immeasurably. My heart is so heavy."

"Let's end now," she said.

We ended the session and I continued to weep.

"Let the tears flow," said Lea, "we can talk to Arjei another time."

Over the next few nights I had insomnia, my mood was somber, and fatigue set in during the day. All I could think about was my mother's miserable life on Earth.

Finally, one night I fell into a deep sleep and dreamed I was in Baltimore, the city where Howard began his career as an assistant rabbi. During the time I was enrolled in college, I'd visited Howard there. He took me to the Inner Harbor, and we toured some historical sites. But in this dream, Howard led me inside the lobby of a grand and luxurious hotel. My mother emerged from the hotel lobby looking young, vibrant, and beautiful. She appeared as if she was in her 30s. Howard guided us through the rooms of this lavish resort. We strolled to the back of the hotel and walked outside through the automatic sliding doors that opened onto a terrace. Nighttime had descended. Through the darkness I could faintly see an outline of cliffs. As we all gingerly walked on ridges of the cliffs, my mother fell into the deep canyon below. I cried out, "Mommy, where are you?" But there was no sound. Not an utterance. Was she dead? Petrified, I bent down to see if she might be clinging to the rocks. No. She'd disappeared into thin air.

I woke up shaking and yelling out loud, "Mommy, what are you trying to tell me? I don't understand!"

Out of nowhere, I heard a soothing voice in my head speak. It said, "I did not scream because I am no longer in pain."

Was that my mother who was speaking? Or was my mind playing tricks?

I wasn't sure but I began to calm down. Then I pledged that I would not host any more pity parties for my mother. This wasn't the first emotional breakdown I'd had, thinking about my mom's tormented life, but I was determined that it would be my last. I decided that if any of those destructive thoughts reappeared, I would focus on the wonderful attributes that I loved most about my mom…like how she instilled confidence in me, and made me believe that I was capable of achieving my dreams, that she trusted in me and would never stay upset with me if I had done something wrong. She always forgave me. Her unconditional love and support were the greatest gifts I had ever received.

Later that week, Lea called to check in on me. I told her about the dream and what had transpired afterwards.

She said, "Of course, that was your mother communicating with you." Lea went on to affirm for me that the spirits of my mom and Howard both came to visit me in my dream. They knew I was in pain and wanted to reassure me that they were doing fine. She said that they were both watching over my children and me.

I felt comforted by Lea's words and told her that I would like one last session with Arjei. We set a date to meet again the following week.

CHAPTER 16

THERE ARE NO SECRETS

ॐ

"Lea, I never imagined that these sessions were going to be so emotional. It's one surprise after another."

"I know that it was difficult listening to Arjei talk about your mother's life. But you're a strong woman, and you always manage to overcome challenging situations."

The quote, 'this too shall pass,' came to my mind. I understand that life has its ups and downs, that navigating difficult situations can bring internal growth, wisdom, and strength—but I was in need of a reprieve.

Lea got quiet and I inhaled a few deep breaths. She recited her prayer and said, "Archangel Michael and Arjei are present. Arjei is very sorry that he caused you distress."

I told Arjei that I appreciated him being straightforward with me all along. When I was young, I survived my childhood trauma by numbing myself emotionally. As an adult, I had spent a good part of my life avoiding conflict and pain. But the pangs of my past always seemed to haunt me. I'd learned to turn toward my suffering, feel the emotion, and then let it all go.

It was especially cathartic writing my memoir even though some of my relatives and friends were appalled that I had broadcasted the abusive nature of my father, being that he was a Holocaust survivor. In my community, Holocaust survivors are revered, yet I felt compelled to write my story because I wanted to have open discussions about the topic of forgiveness. Many of my readers expressed their gratitude that I'd come forward because they, too, were children of survivors or who also grew up in abusive homes and were grateful to know that they were not alone. I had written my memoir in hope that others who had also been abused, neglected, abandoned, and harassed as children and adults by family, friends, and co-workers might learn a way to heal.

Arjei said, "When your mom died, I was happy for her. She was finally free from your dad and no longer trapped. I tried my best to comfort your mom, but she could not hear or sense me. Every time I yelled at your dad to stop hurting her, the voices inside of him confused him."

I sat there listening and taking notes while Arjei continued: "Eventually, I realized that I could never leave his body, so I surrendered. I became an observer, but I could still sense his emotions and sensations. Like I said, I turned away when he did awful things. But you Karen, you could sense me. In fact, you have seen me."

"I've seen you?"

"Yes. In your parents' wedding picture."

"Oh my God!" I exclaimed, "that's you? I thought it was the devil!" I sat there wide-eyed with my mouth open.

Lea asked, "What are you talking about?"

"I wanted to include a picture of my parents in my memoir. Hanging in my hallway is an 11 x 14 wedding portrait of my parents, taken in 1954."

Lea said, "Yes, I've seen the picture in your home. Your dad was extremely handsome, and your mom was beautiful."

"When I used my iPhone to snap a photo of the portrait, I noticed a silhouette of a man's face above my father. He has a full head of dark hair and a long, thick, pointed black beard. His eyes are piercing down at my father with a sinister look. It creeped me out, so I took down the picture from the wall and stored it in a closet for a few months."

"That isn't the devil, it's me," said Arjei.

"I can't believe that!" I exclaimed. I sat there in wonder trying to grasp this beyond-belief moment.

Lea said, "You have had incredible experiences, Karen, and I hope you're putting them into another book."

"But who would believe this story?" I thought. It is unfathomable.

Wedding portrait of Harriet and Arie Kaplan.

Lea asked, "What are your final questions for today?"

I looked at my notes and sat upright as I was trying to refocus on today's session. "Arjei, can you explain why my father intentionally cut me out of the will? I found an updated will after my mom had died which stated that upon the death of my father, my brother would inherit the majority of his estate. Yet when my mom was alive, my parents agreed that Barry and I would split the inheritance. Something happened that made my dad change his mind, years later."

Arjei said, "Your dad was angry that you had divorced. You embarrassed him and broke up the family. He felt it was a reflection on him. He was determined to never give up in the face of adversity. It is a test of character. He persevered through great hardships and yours were minuscule in comparison."

I remembered when I approached the subject of divorce with my dad. I told him that I had made a major decision.

He pointed and waved his index finger at me and said, "Don't do it!"

I told him that I didn't love my husband anymore.

He didn't care. He was incensed and said, "That's no excuse. Don't bother coming to me for money if you need help. I won't give you any." He warned me several more times, but I wasn't going to live my life for anyone else anymore. In January of 2003, I went to sign the official divorce papers at the Daley Center in downtown Chicago. My father fumed the day it became official. I was proud of myself.

During the last few years of his life when I'd drive him to doctor appointments, the banks and grocery stores, I remember asking if my name should be added on all his bank statements, alongside my brother's name. He had agreed. Also, at that time my father began paying for my lunch when we stopped on Devon Avenue at a kosher restaurant. I think he was softening up a bit as he was aging.

"Any final questions?" asked Lea.

"Yes," I said, but then I felt compelled to share a story: my father's final week of life.

During one of the morning visits to the nursing home, I found my father unresponsive and struggling to breathe. I called for an ambulance and he was rushed to Highland Park Hospital. He lay in a coma, on a ventilator for a week, in the intensive care unit. My father was 89 years old at that time.

In recent months, he had lost so much weight that his shoulder bones and ribs were protruding from his body. His eyes were deeply sunken into the sockets, his face was gaunt, and his skin had a grayish tint. In the ICU, his arms were bruised from the IVs and his hands and feet were swollen with fluid. He had severe edema. The doctor had said that his organs were shutting down and together we decided to remove him from the ventilator.

Once he was off the ventilator, I'd visit him in the ICU and sit quietly in the corner of his room while the doctor and nurses were making their rounds. On the seventh morning of this routing, something changed inside of me. For the first time, I felt compassion in my heart for my father.

I walked over to his bedside and sat next to his near-lifeless body. I brushed the hair off his forehead so that I could see his full face and noticed two vertical lines between his brows. It seemed like he was in pain. Then I held his swollen hand in mine and said, "Daddy, let go. You've suffered your entire life…there's no need to suffer in death. Free yourself from this pain. Please let go. Your father Chaim Shlomo, your mother, Beila, your sisters, Yoshpe, Chaya Esther, Leah, and Gitel, along with your baby brother, Yehuda Leizer, are all waiting for you. Let go daddy, just let go."

My eyes welled with tears that trickled down my cheeks and dropped onto the sheet. I cried for several minutes. I wiped my tears away and looked up at my father and said, "Daddy, I forgive you. I want you to know that I honestly forgive you."

At that moment, his eyes popped wide open!

I was startled. I leaned to the right and he tracked me. Then as I moved to the left, his eyes continued following me. I thought that if anyone could cheat death, it would be him. He was a fighter and a survivor.

I ran out of the room to the nurses' station, yelling that my father was finally waking up. When the nurse and I returned, my father's eyes were closed once again.

He died the next morning.

I asked Arjei, "I always wondered what my dad was thinking at that moment. Did he understand what I was saying? Was he trying to respond? Many people on their deathbed often apologize for the hurt they caused and will confess their wrongdoings."

Arjei said, "I'm sorry to say but your father heard you and was fuming. When you spoke of forgiveness, he felt you were coming from a place of weakness. Weakness is not part of his vocabulary. When he took advantage and preyed upon the frail and feeble minded, it made him feel powerful.

"He watched his family be murdered and thought you had *chutzpah* to accuse him of any wrongdoings! He survived the war, and as a result, brought you into this world. He gave you life."

My body went numb. I was shocked and disheartened once again. I sat there dwelling on Arjei's comments.

"What are you thinking?" asked Lea.

"I guess I was a bit hopeful, or maybe I'm just so naive to think that my dad might have changed on his deathbed."

Arjei said, "Don't think of your dad as a monster. He suffered incredibly. He loved his family in Poland and watching them be murdered was more than he could bear. He was tormented all these years.

"When he was in his 40s and 50s, your dad had excruciating pain throughout his body and became addicted to painkillers. His body had never recovered from those years of starvation and malnutrition. The pain medication made him mean and irritable and he secluded himself in his bedroom. Your mother felt all alone. He could never be vulnerable again and had very little empathy for anyone. He never felt loved but loved his people and Howard the most. He did his best and provided for your family. I tried to influence your dad by telling him that strength comes from kindness of the heart. I wanted him to respect and not bully others. I wanted him to do the right thing. But he never listened. In his quiet moments, he was anguished and mentally tortured. After Howard died, he knew that he got a raw deal in life and continued his rampage of abuse toward your mother."

"I cannot imagine living his life," I said.

"When your dad died, I was free. We both ascended in our spirit. It felt like a balloon that had been set free. It was a strange sensation and I was relieved to be out of your father's energy field. I have vowed to never let myself attach to anyone else and have learned my lesson. My parents came for me and I was surprised to see them. I didn't know what to expect. Your dad continues to remain in a fragile state on the other side," said Arjei. "I hope I have given you clarity about your father."

I said to Arjei, "You have given me more clarity than I ever expected. I'm sincerely grateful for our time together. I am truly honored to have befriended you. Arjei, I wish you an after-life of happiness." I knew I was going to miss this beautiful soul and that he would forever be ingrained in my heart.

Arjei said, "Good-bye my friend, and thank you for all that you have done for me."

That was the last time we communicated.

CHAPTER 17

CHANCE OR FATE?

ॐ

I thought about the juxtaposition of my father's and Arjei's life. By chance, my father came upon Arjei, the dead soldier, that one fateful morning in the woods. Searching through Arjei's clothes, my father found his *mischling* identification card, revealing that Arjei had come from Rajgròd, coincidentally from the other town in Poland with that name. By assuming his alias, my dad felt that he could thwart the men who murdered his family from ever finding him. It also permitted my father to maneuver his way through the countryside, giving him leverage over the villagers so that he would be provided with food and necessities. This German army identification would have been useful had he been caught by the Nazis. Arjei's identification offered peace of mind for my father, and a lifeline for his survival during the Holocaust.

Arjei and my father were both victims of Hitler's nefarious world war on humanity.

Arjei Kaplan was conscripted into an army that annihilated many of his family members and his community. When he learned the hidden truth, he resolved to escape from the world's most powerful army. Despite his impediment and knowing his life was at risk, he fled from Auschwitz into the forests. This act of defiance was monumental and heroic. So many German soldiers complied and actively participated in heinous acts of genocide.

Anyone can be a soldier, anyone can learn to shoot and kill, but few soldiers had Arjei's courage to defy The Third Reich.

Traumatized after witnessing the horrendous murder of his mother and sisters, my father Avrum Szteinsaper escaped into those same forests of Europe where he unjustly suffered for three-and-a-half years while evading the German army. Malnourished, traumatized, and hunted by Nazis with guard dogs, wild animals, and locals from the villages, he never succumbed to death and miraculously survived.

Arjei died with fury in his heart while my father, Avrum/Arie, lived with anger in his heart. Together, like conjoined twins, they shared a toxic energy field for 70 years.

Arjei's energy contributed to my father's volatile disposition and exasperated his internal make-up. Once Arjei realized that he could no longer uncage himself from my father's auric field, he resigned himself to becoming a spectator and he let go of his anger. Each time my father lashed out onto my family, Arjei turned away. His kind intentions to console my mother were unsuccessful. Arjei tried to reason with my father but to no avail; he could not be helped. The hardships of the war had seared my father emotionally, yet Arjei tried to be my father's conscience.

Arjei may not have realized that his physical death was the key to keeping my father alive. In a way, Arjei the soldier sacrificed his life to allow my father and generations of my family to continue. His death was not in vain.

Communicating with Arjei through Lea led me to a greater understanding of my father, myself, and the spiritual world. Arjei's insight was an incredible gift—the gift of a lifetime. I also learned that healing doesn't end with death; rather, one can continue to send loving thoughts and prayers to those whose bodies have died. This world has so many levels of consciousness, yet we are all connected to one another.

In the future, I plan to return to Poland and visit Arjei's birthplace, the city of Ostrowo and look up his family records. I'd also like to visit his hometown—the other Rajgròd.

There is a Jewish custom to light memorial candles for departed family members three times a year during the Jewish holidays. Every year I light one candle for my mother, father, and brother Howard. Then I light an additional one for all my family members who perished in the Holocaust. This year, I've added a candle for Arjei.

Arjei's family lineage ceased when his entire family was murdered during the war. He was extremely concerned that his family name might be shamed as he divulged his story through Lea. Yet all I have is pride, respect, and gratitude for him and feel privileged to have communicated with him. My surname, Kaplan, is indeed a noble name and now that the mystery of my father's alias has been solved, I will carry on the name Kaplan with integrity and honor.

May Arjei Kaplan, and my father, Arie Kaplan (Avrum Szteinsaper) both rest in peace and may their memories be of a blessing.

THE END

ACKNOWLEDGMENTS

It was *beshert* [fate] that Mary L. Holden became my editor. I am greatly indebted to her and grateful for all the time and energy she spent working on this book.

To all my friends, *shvesters* [sisters], and family who took the time to read various chapters and provide feedback, thank you.

To my husband Bobby, my soulmate, who unknowingly tempers me with his love, patience, kindness and calm…who listened to each chapter rewrite at all hours of the day and night. Thank you.

To my children Raquel, Noah, Max, his wife Michelle, and their baby Braeden. You inspire me to follow my passions. My heart is full of love for all of you.

In memory of my dear brother, Howard, who showed me that strength comes from the goodness of the heart. You were my childhood protector and I am thankful that you continue to guide me in spirit.

To my mom—forever in my heart. You are my rock and role model. You showed me how to love unconditionally. Until we meet in the afterlife, I will continue to miss you each and every day.

With appreciation for my father Arie, who taught me one of my most invaluable lessons…learning to forgive.

To my spirit friend, Arjei Kaplan, thank you for having courage to come forward and share your life story with me.

I'm so grateful to Lea Chapin, my therapist, teacher, and friend. Through your kindness, Lea, and your compassion and wisdom, I was able to bring this story to life.

ABOUT THE AUTHOR

Karen Kaplan was born and raised in West Rogers Park, a Jewish neighborhood on the north side of Chicago. After publishing her first memoir, *Descendants of Rajgròd: Learning To Forgive*, Karen has been engaging audiences worldwide. She continues to share her compelling life story and the message of forgiveness.

After receiving a B.A. from the University of Illinois in Nutrition and Medical Dietetics Karen trained at The Claret Center of Hyde Park, IL as a spiritual director.

Articles, excerpts, and news stories of Karen's first book have been featured on WGN-TV Chicago morning news, on Bialystok TV news, German, and local cable and radio shows, *The New Yorker, The Bronx Times, The Chicago Jewish News, Chicago JUF News, The Skokie Review, Deerfield Review,* the *Highland Park Highlander,* and *Highland Park Landmark.*

Karen has developed a feature-length screenplay based on her memoir that was selected for The Hemingway Award at the Los Angeles Live Film Festival in November 2021 and selected for the Eastern European Festival in Warsaw December 2020.

She is determined to bring this story to the big screen.

KarenLKaplan.com

Karenkaplan@att.net